PARTY-PERFECT BITES

PARTY-PERFECT BITES

delicious recipes for
canapés, finger food
and party snacks

MILLI TAYLOR

photography by
Helen Cathcart

rps

RYLAND PETERS & SMALL
LONDON • NEW YORK

To Mum and Dad, for raising me with such
a healthy appetite for all good things in life.

For more information about Milli's catering,
see www.milliscatering.co.uk

Designer *Barbara Zuñiga*
Editor *Kate Eddison*
Production Controller *Sarah Kulasek-Boyd*
Art Director *Leslie Harrington*
Editorial Director *Julia Charles*
Publisher *Cindy Richards*

Food Stylist *Milli Taylor*
Prop Stylist *Jo Harris*
Indexer *Hilary Bird*

First published in 2014.
This revised edition published in 2019 by
Ryland Peters & Small
20–21 Jockey's Fields
London WC1R 4BW
and
341 E 116th St
New York NY 10029

www.rylandpeters.com

Text © Milli Taylor 2014, 2019
Design and photographs
© Ryland Peters & Small 2014, 2019

ISBN: 978-1-78879-157-1

10 9 8 7 6 5 4 3 2 1

Printed and bound in China

Notes
• Both British (metric) and American (ounces plus
US cups) are included in these recipes for your
convenience, however it is important to work with
one set of measurements and not alternate between
the two within a recipe.
• All spoon measurements are level, unless otherwise
specified.
• All herbs used in these recipes are fresh, unless
otherwise specified.
• All eggs are large (UK) or extra-large (US), unless
otherwise stated.
• When a recipe calls for the grated zest of citrus
fruit, buy unwaxed fruit and wash well before using.
If you can only find treated fruit, scrub well in warm
soapy water before using.
• Ovens should be preheated to the specified
temperatures. We recommend using an oven
thermometer. Recipes were tested using a
fan-assisted oven.

contents

planning a party

I cook all sorts of food for different events, but my most positive feedback is always from my canapé parties. Don't get me wrong; a classic devilled egg will always go down a treat, and who doesn't love a cheese straw? However, it does feel about time we shook things up a bit and got more adventurous with our party food.

I've taken inspiration from supper clubs to street food and everything in-between. I hope in this book I can introduce you to some new flavours and ingredients and you'll have as much fun creating them as your guests have eating them.

What should a canapé be?

* Bite-sized – they should be easy to eat.
* Full of flavour – make that one mouthful pack a punch.
* Fun – don't get worked up about what's authentic and correct; this is the time to play around with flavours.

We eat with our eyes

Canapés should look appetizing. You can go the whole hog with the micro-herbs and fancy toppings, or keep the food simple and decorate your plate.

Not every plate of food has to have decoration, although a garnish can help indicate what is in the canapé. For example, if I'm serving some spicy fishcakes I may put a bunch of fresh coriander/cilantro and chilli/chile on the side of the plate.

Sometimes simple is best. If your food looks intricate and pretty, let it stand alone on a plain white plate.

Think beyond your kitchen plates. A banana leaf polished with a little vegetable oil can look lovely with tropical food on it. You can use anything from tin serving trays to chopping boards, as long as they are clean and food safe. But think practically. Your plates need to have a flat surface so your creations don't fall over and they should be light enough to hand around. If you're serving skewers, make sure there is an empty pot or glass for people to dispose of their used skewers.

Planning your party

Some of us are planners, some of us are not. Some love a spreadsheet, while others just hope it will all be alright on the night. Even if you fall into the latter camp, be aware that the more you plan and do ahead, the less you will have to do on the day, and the more fun you can have at your own party.

There are three main aspects to party planning:
* What food you are going to serve.
* What your guests are going to drink.
* The other stuff...

What food will you serve?
Quantity

If you are thinking of serving pre-meal canapés, perhaps as an alternative to a starter, then you should allow three to five canapés per person.

For a drinks party of around three hours, I would offer 11 canapés per head. You could start with a few canapés, then offer bowl food to ease the workload.

There does not have to be a different variety for each canapé. For example, if you wanted to provide 12 canapés per head, it could be four types, three of each. I tend to cater for at least one and a half of each canapé per person, so that if someone takes two, another person won't go without.

Choosing which canapés to prepare

Pick a mix of hot and cold bites, including some things you can make ahead. Balance the menu in terms of fresh/fried, light/filling and different flavours. Offer a variety of fish, shellfish, meat, poultry and vegetable canapés. Use local and seasonal ingredients, not only to reduce the food miles, but because they cost less and taste better.

Be generous. You may not cook each of your guests a fillet steak/beef tenderloin for dinner, but at a canapé party, just one steak can make 20 canapés. It feels like a luxury to be offered prawns/shrimp, fillet steak/beef tenderloin or caviar, even if in such small quantities.

If you know good store-bought products that can make your life easier, use them. Always. No one expects everything you offer to be home-made. I often order miniature bagels from

my local bakery, and if throwing something impromptu, I will pick up some mini croustades from the shop and fill them at home with something fresh and delicious.

Will anyone be bringing children? Keep kids happy with mini sandwiches, crudités and cocktail sausages.

Don't forget dessert! You would end a dinner on a sweet note, so do the same with canapés. Last impressions are as important as first ones.

What will your guests be drinking?

Running out of booze at a party is a real no-no. To ensure this doesn't happen, buy more than you think you need, by purchasing from a company with a sale-or-return option. Many companies also offer free delivery and free glass and ice bucket hire with a deposit.

If you are sticking to a budget, here are my tips:
* Consider pitchers of cocktails or spritzers in the summer, and mulled wine in the winter.
* Use Champagne for toasts and then Cava or Prosecco for refills.
* Look for deals a few weeks before the party – some don't stick around for long.

Don't forget the soft drinks

People who are not drinking alcohol shouldn't be made to feel left out, so provide an interesting 'mocktail' or a sparkling elderflower pressé that can be used for a toast in a flute.

Ice

If you have no refrigerator space for drinks, then use large plastic ice buckets to chill drinks.

Buy and arrange a delivery of ice. Maybe not if you have a short guest list, but it's good not to have to think about it, and terrible if you run out.

The other stuff not to forget

There's a lot to think about when catering for large numbers at home. With moving furniture, cleaning, drinks and cooking, accept help when offered!

You may want to do all the cooking yourself, but hiring waiting staff or bar staff makes life easier.

Getting friends to lend a hand in the kitchen or serving drinks is also a must. If I have a friend who doesn't know many people, I'll ask him or her to hand around a plate of canapés – an easy way to approach guests and make quick introductions.

Many of the following tasks can be done early in the planning process.
* Invitations – it sounds obvious, but make sure your guests know that you will be providing food. Then they can let you know if they have any food intolerances. It is best to have a few vegetarian and gluten-free options anyway.
* Music – make a playlist, or use a sharing app.
* Transportation – make sure you have a local taxi number written somewhere that people can see.
* Coats – will guests be wearing coats when they arrive? It may be worth buying a cheap, collapsible rail or just making sure you have a bed made up on which you can pile them.
* Neighbours – advise (or invite?) the neighbours. If they know what time you are finishing there will be less reason for them to feel disgruntled.
* Buy napkins, toilet paper and rubbish bags.
* A day or so before the party, clear out your refrigerator to maximize the space. You need to be mindful of leaving food unchilled for too long.

A note on all recipes.

If you are doubling or tripling recipes, be aware that you may not need to multiply your seasonings and dips in the same way as your base ingredients. For example, for lamb skewers you will need to double the lamb, but perhaps just stick to one quantity of marinade or dipping sauce.

Helpful tools

* Measuring spoons – it's very important in some recipes to make sure the measures are precise.
* A 24-hole mini muffin tray.
* Non-stick silicone mats.
* Disposable piping/pastry bags.
* A sugar/candy thermometer. If you don't have a deep-fryer, a thermometer is useful in keeping your oil at the right temperature for frying.

Dips & Dippers

It really isn't a party without dips! Fill a tray
with an array of colourful dips, crackers and
crudités. They are easy to prepare ahead
and any early arrivals can be kept happy
while you nip back into the kitchen.

romesco dip

6 tomatoes, halved

4 red/bell peppers, halved and deseeded

6 tablespoons olive oil

50 g/generous ⅓ cup hazelnuts or
almonds, blanched

15-cm/6-in. piece of stale white
baguette/French bread,
broken into chunks

3 garlic cloves

1 tablespoon sherry vinegar

½ teaspoon smoked paprika

salt and freshly ground black pepper

Makes 800 g/1¾ lbs.

Preheat the oven to 200°C (400°F) Gas 6.

Place the tomatoes and peppers in separate roasting pans, season with salt and pepper, then drizzle 1 tablespoon of the olive oil over each pan. Roast in the preheated oven for about 35 minutes, or until the skins on the peppers have started to blacken.

Meanwhile, blitz the blanched nuts in a food processor or blender.

Remove the tomatoes from the pan and set aside. Add the chunks of baguette/French bread to the tomato juices in the pan. Let cool.

Remove the peppers from the pan and place into a bowl. Cover with clingfilm/plastic wrap, and let cool.

Once cooled, remove and discard the skins from the peppers and add the peppers to the food processor along with the tomatoes. Add the remaining 4 tablespoons of olive oil, along with the garlic, soaked bread, sherry vinegar and smoked paprika. Blitz until smooth. Season with salt to taste, then serve.

guacamole

6 ripe Hass avocados, halved
and stoned/pitted

½ red onion, finely chopped

a handful of freshly chopped
coriander/cilantro

2 red chillies/chiles, finely chopped

freshly squeezed juice of 2 limes

2–3 pinches of sea salt flakes

Tabasco and cayenne pepper (optional)

Makes 700 g/25 oz.

Scoop the flesh out of the avocado with a tablespoon into a shallow bowl. Add the onion, coriander/cilantro and chillies/chiles.

Add the lime juice, then mash everything together with a fork, leaving the texture quite chunky.

Season with salt to taste. Add a few dashes of Tabasco and sprinkle with cayenne, if you like. Serve with tortilla chips (see page 16).

crudités

**A selection of crudités is a quick and colourful addition to any nibbles party.
I like to use crisp and fresh baby carrots, sliced sweet/bell peppers and
cucumber sticks, as well as blanched asparagus and green beans.**

beetroot hummus

140 g/1 cup canned chickpeas,
  drained and rinsed
250 g/2 scant cups beetroot/beets,
  cooked and cubed
1 large garlic clove
2 tablespoons olive oil

1 tablespoon freshly squeezed
  lemon juice
2 tablespoons tahini
2–3 pinches of sea salt flakes

Makes 400 g/14 oz.

Place all of the ingredients in a food processor or blender and blitz until smooth. Taste and adjust the seasoning, if necessary.

blue cheese dip

150 g/scant ¾ cup Greek/
  US strained plain yogurt
150 ml/scant ¾ cup sour cream
90 g/generous ¾ cup blue cheese,
  such as Stilton or Gorgonzola
3 tablespoons mayonnaise
a pinch of salt

a splash of Worcestershire sauce or
  freshly squeezed lemon juice
1 tablespoon chopped/snipped
  chives, plus extra for decoration

Makes 400 g/14 oz.

Place all of the ingredients except the chives in a food processor or blender, and blitz until smooth.

Transfer to a serving bowl and stir in the chopped/snipped chives. Sprinkle some extra chives on top for decoration.

squid ink crackers

Squid ink creates a very dramatic black colour in these crackers. It is available in convenient sachets from Italian and Spanish specialist stores, and from some online retailers.

300 g/2¼ cups plain/
  all-purpose flour
1 teaspoon baking powder
1 teaspoon salt
½ teaspoon cayenne pepper
80 ml/⅓ cup olive oil
3 x 4-g/⅙-oz. squid ink sachets

a baking sheet, lined with
baking parchment

Makes 15

Preheat the oven to 180°C (350°F) Gas 4.

Mix the flour, baking powder, salt and cayenne pepper in a large mixing bowl, and make a well in the middle.

Mix 150 ml/⅔ cup water with the olive oil and squid ink, then add to the well. Stir gently, slowly incorporating the dry ingredients until a dough forms.

Turn out the dough onto a floured surface, and knead for about 3–5 minutes, or until smooth. Divide the dough into 15 pieces and roll them into the desired shapes with a rolling pin.

Transfer the shapes to the prepared baking sheet and bake for about 10–15 minutes in the preheated oven, or until crisp on the undersides. Cool on a wire rack. Keep in an airtight container for up to 3 days before serving.

This page: beetroot hummus (p13), squid ink crackers (p13).
Opposite: guacamole (p12), romesco dip (p12), blue cheese
dip (p13), crudités (p12).

tzatziki

1 large, firm cucumber
½ teaspoon salt
400 g/2 scant cups Greek/
US strained plain yogurt
2 tablespoons freshly chopped dill,
plus extra to garnish (optional)
2 garlic cloves, crushed
2 pinches of salt
1 tablespoon olive oil

Makes 500 g/1 lb 2oz.

Peel, deseed and dice the cucumber. Sprinkle it with the salt, mix well and set aside for 5 minutes.

Wrap the cucumber in a clean kitchen towel and squeeze to remove the liquid from the cucumber.

Place the cucumber in a bowl and add the remaining ingredients. Mix together well and serve, garnished with dill, if you like.

roast carrot, ginger & miso dip

300 g/10½ oz. carrots, peeled
and thinly sliced
25 g/1 oz. grated ginger
3 tablespoons white miso paste
2 tablespoons tahini
sesame seeds, to garnish
(optional)

Makes 350 g/12 oz.

Preheat the oven to 180°C (350°F) Gas 4.

Place the carrots in a roasting pan and roast in the preheated oven for 20–25 minutes until softened. Set aside until cool.

Blitz the cooled carrots in a food processor or blender together with the ginger, miso and tahini. Serve, sprinkled with sesame seeds, if desired.

tortilla chips

8 soft wheat flour tortillas
sunflower or vegetable oil

Makes 1 big bowl

Stack the tortillas and cut into even triangles, like a pizza.

Pour about 2.5 cm/1 in. of oil into a small saucepan and put over medium-high heat.

When the oil is hot, test-fry one triangle. It should take about 30 seconds for the first side to become crisp. (Use tongs or a slotted spoon to turn the tortilla over to fry the other side.)

Fry the tortillas in batches and, when golden brown, drain on paper towels. When cool, store in an airtight container until ready to use.

artichoke & spinach dip

80 g/3 oz. spinach, washed
1 x 280-g/10-oz. jar
  artichoke hearts in oil
  (170 g/6 oz. drained
  weight)
20 g/1 oz. Boursin or other
  garlic and herb soft cheese

40 g/2 oz. grated Parmesan
80 g/3 oz. sour cream or
  crème fraîche
freshly ground black pepper

Makes 350 g/12 oz.

Blitz the spinach in a food processor or blender.

Drain the artichoke hearts and add them to the food processor or blender, together with all the remaining ingredients.

Season to taste with freshly ground pepper.

---

black bean hummus

1 x 400-g/14-oz. can of
  black beans (240 g/
  8½ oz. drained weight)
½ teaspoon freshly chopped
  coriander/cilantro
1½ teaspoons cumin
freshly squeezed juice of
  1 lime
1 tablespoon tahini

1 large garlic clove, crushed
1 teaspoon smoked paprika
½ teaspoon cayenne pepper,
  plus extra to garnish
1 tablespoon olive oil, plus
  extra to drizzle
2 pinches of sea salt flakes

Makes 450 g/1 lb.

Reserve a few beans and a couple of coriander/cilantro leaves to garnish, then blitz the remaining ingredients in a food processor or blender, together with 3 tablespoons of water.

Garnish with the reserved coriander/cilantro, beans, a drizzle of olive oil and a sprinkle of cayenne.

---

marinated feta

You'll need to make this at least a day ahead. You can pop whatever you like in the oil – from chillies/chiles to pink peppercorns. Make sure you serve tortilla chips or chunks of bread to spoon the cheese on.

400 g/14 oz. feta cheese,
  cut into small chunks
400 ml/1¾ cups good-quality
  olive oil
grated zest of 1 lemon
1 tablespoon fennel seeds
1 red onion, thinly sliced
3 sprigs thyme or rosemary

Makes 400 g/14 oz.

Put all the ingredients in a sterilized jar and pop it in the refrigerator for a few days. If you only have a night, warm the oil with everything except the cheese in a pan. Let it cool, then add the cheese and refrigerate, until you are ready to serve.

Serve with a spoon to remove the feta from the oil.

Overleaf clockwise from left: tzatziki (p16), roast carrot, ginger & miso dip (p16), tortilla chips (p16), artichoke & spinach dip (p17), black bean hummus (p17), marinated feta (p17), baba ganoush (p98).

spicy popcorn

100 g/3½ oz. corn kernels
2 tablespoons sunflower oil
50 g/3 tablespoons unsalted
* butter, melted*
½ teaspoon salt
½ teaspoon paprika
* (smoked is good)*
¼ teaspoon cayenne pepper

1 large lidded saucepan at least
24 cm/9½ in. in diameter and
13 cm/5 in. deep

Makes 1 large bowl

Put the corn and the oil into a pan and spread the kernels out to make an even layer. Cover with a lid and cook over medium-high heat.

When the kernels start popping, shake the pan a few times to distribute the heat. The kernels will only take a few minutes to cook.

Put the popcorn into a large bowl and drizzle over the melted butter. Finally sprinkle with the salt, paprika and cayenne pepper, toss well and serve.

stilton & walnut biscuits

180 g/1½ cups plain/
* all-purpose flour*
90 g/6 tablespoons unsalted
* butter, at room temperature*
a pinch of salt
90 g/3 oz. Stilton or other blue
* cheese, crumbled*
1 egg, beaten
50 g/½ cup walnut halves

a baking sheet, lined with
baking parchment

Makes 30

Put the flour, butter, salt and Stilton in a food processor or blender and pulse until well combined. Add ice-cold water, a teaspoonful at a time, if needed, to bring the ingredients together.

Tip out the dough onto a floured surface and roll into a log, 1 cm/½ in. thick. Wrap in clingfilm/plastic wrap and leave in the refrigerator for at least 1 hour. You can keep the dough in the refrigerator for a week before cooking or freeze ahead of time.

Preheat the oven to 180°C (350°F) Gas 4.

Slice the log into 6-mm/¼-in disks and lay them out on the prepared baking sheet, allowing space for the disks to spread. Brush the tops with the beaten egg and add a walnut half.

Bake in the preheated oven for 12–15 minutes. Let cool on a wire rack, then store in an airtight container or freeze for up to 2 weeks.

antipasti

Although antipasti is an Italian concept, I use a mixture of Mediterranean nibbles, such as chorizo, salami, prosciutto, grissini, Manchego cheese, marinated artichoke hearts, olives, cherry tomatoes and banderillas.

cayenne & cheddar biscuits

200 g/1⅔ cup plain/
*   all-purpose flour*
130 g/1 stick plus 1 tablespoon
*   unsalted butter, cubed*
180 g/6 oz. Cheddar cheese,
*   grated*
1 teaspoon cayenne pepper
½ teaspoon smoked paprika
a pinch of salt
poppy seeds, to decorate

a baking sheet, lined with
baking parchment

Makes 40

Put all the ingredients into a food processor or blender and blitz until well combined. If the dough doesn't come together when pinched, add 1 tablespoon cold water and blitz again.

Put the dough into a bowl and knead into a ball.

Tip the dough out onto a lightly floured surface, and roll out into a log 4 cm/1½ in. in diameter. Cut in half. Wrap in clingfilm/plastic wrap and chill for at least 1 hour.

Preheat the oven to 180°C (350°F) Gas 4.

Roll the logs in the poppy seeds, if using. Slice each log into 20 disks and transfer them to the prepared baking sheet.

(Alternatively, roll each half of dough into a 12 x 34-cm/5 x 13½-in. rectangle and cut each rectangle into 20 sticks. Sprinkle the poppy seeds onto the sticks and transfer to the baking sheet.)

Bake in the preheated oven for 14–15 minutes, until golden and the edges are brown. Let cool on a wire rack, then store in an airtight container or freeze for up to 2 weeks.

....

madras cheddar biscuits

120 g/1 cup plain/
*   all-purpose flour*
80 g/5 tablespoons unsalted
*   butter, chopped*
120 g/4 oz. Cheddar cheese,
*   grated*
½ teaspoon salt
2 teaspoons mild madras
*   curry powder*
cumin seeds, to decorate
*   (optional)*

a baking sheet, lined with
baking parchment

Makes 30

Put all the ingredients into a food processor or blender and blitz until the mixture resembles breadcrumbs. Add 1 tablespoon of cold water, if needed, to bring the ingredients together.

Put the dough into a bowl and work it a little until it forms a ball.

Tip the dough out onto a floured surface. Roll the dough into a sausage approximately 4 cm/1½ in. in diameter.

Wrap in clingfilm/plastic wrap and chill for at least 1 hour.

Preheat the oven to 180°C (350°F) Gas 4.

Slice the dough into 30 pieces and transfer to the prepared baking sheet. Bake in the preheated oven for 12–14 minutes, until golden and the edges are brown. Let cool on a wire rack, then store in an airtight container or freeze for up to 2 weeks.

Pages 24–25, clockwise from left: cayenne & cheddar biscuits (sticks and rounds, p20), tortilla chips (p16), madras cheddar biscuits (p21), anise crackers (p44), squid ink crackers (p13), stilton & walnut biscuits (p20).

This page: Antipasti (p20).
Opposite: Spicy popcorn
(p20).

Mediterranean

My family lives in Spain, and while our lunches aren't the long, lazy kind you see in films, there is definitely a more relaxed approach to cooking and entertaining. This is why some of my recipes in this chapter are more a matter of assembly than cooking.

ajo blanco

This chilled white soup is a traditional dish from southern Spain. Juan, my brother's friend, kindly shared his recipe, which I first tasted at a wedding he catered.

300 g/2¼ cups whole
  almonds, skins on
300 g/5¼ cups white
  breadcrumbs
4 garlic cloves
150–200 ml/⅔–¾ cup
  olive oil
4 tablespoons Jerez sherry
  vinegar
1 teaspoon salt
2 ripe figs, thinly sliced
balsamic reduction, to serve

about 25 shot glasses

**Makes about 25
(1.3 litres/5½ cups)**

Put the almonds into a shallow bowl and cover with boiling water. After a couple of minutes, lift them out, and remove and discard the skins.

Put 600 ml/2½ cups of cold water in a blender. Add the breadcrumbs, garlic, olive oil, vinegar and almonds. Blend until smooth. Add 200 ml/¾ cup cold water and blend until silky. Add extra water if needed to achieve a drinkable consistency. Add the salt, stir well and chill.

To serve, pour the soup into shot glasses. Top with a slice of fig and a drizzle of balsamic reduction.

gazpacho

This really is more of a salmorejo; gazpacho's thicker, creamier cousin.

1 kg/2¼ lbs. ripe tomatoes
1 thick slice of white bread,
  torn into pieces
3 garlic cloves
3 tablespoons extra-virgin
  olive oil
1 teaspoon salt
1 red/bell pepper
1–2 teaspoons sugar
2 tablespoons sherry vinegar
1 slice of jamón Serrano and
  1 hard-boiled/hard-cooked
  egg, chopped, to garnish

about 20 shot glasses

**Makes about 20
(1.3 litres/5½ cups)**

Blitz the tomatoes in a blender and push pieces of the bread down into the juice. Let sit for 5 minutes.

Blend again with all the remaining ingredients until smooth. Chill in the refrigerator.

To serve, mix the soup well, pour into shot glasses and garnish with the chopped egg and chopped jamón Serrano.

crostini

Using part-baked baguettes allows you to slice thin and neat crostini.

2 part-baked baguettes, each
  sliced into 30–35 slices about
  5-mm/¼-inch thick
100 ml/scant ½ cup olive oil

Makes 60–70

Heat a griddle pan on high and brush each side of the bread with olive oil.

Cook the bread, in batches, for 1 minute on each side, until the bread is toasted and crisp. Remove and place onto a wire rack to cool. Alternatively, bake them on a baking sheet in an oven at 180°C (350°F) Gas 4 for 8–10 minutes.

broad bean, ricotta & feta crostini with pancetta

10 slices/strips pancetta

300 g/2¼ cups frozen petits pois

200 g/1¼ cups broad/fava beans,
  fresh or frozen

1 tablespoon olive oil

grated zest of ½ lemon

100 g/3½ oz. ricotta

10 freshly chopped mint leaves,
  plus 10 leaves, to garnish

salt and freshly ground black pepper

40 crostini (see opposite)

200 g/7 oz. feta, crumbled

Makes 40

Preheat the oven to 180°C (350°F) Gas 4.

Cut each slice/strip of pancetta crossways into 4.

Put the pancetta onto a baking sheet and bake in the preheated oven for 10 minutes, or until crisp. Drain any excess fat on paper towels and set aside.

Put the frozen petits pois in a pan of boiling water for 1 minute and then plunge into cold water. Repeat with the beans and then squeeze them out of their skins.

Put the petits pois and half of the beans into a food processor or blender. Blend together with the olive oil, lemon zest, ricotta, mint, salt and pepper.

Spread a teaspoonful of the mix on top of each crostini, followed by a little feta, chopped mint, remaining beans and piece of pancetta. Serve.

mediterranean vegetable crostini with pesto

4 tablespoons olive oil

1 red/bell pepper

½ aubergine/eggplant, thinly sliced

1 courgette/zucchini, thinly sliced

¼ red onion, cut into wedges
  (optional)

1 x 125-g/4½-oz. mozzarella ball

40 crostini (see opposite)

For the pesto

50 g/generous ⅓ cup pine nuts

40 g/1½ oz. fresh basil leaves

1 garlic clove

60 g/1 cup freshly grated
  Parmesan

3 tablespoons olive oil

a squeeze of lemon juice

freshly ground black pepper

Makes 40

Preheat the oven to 200°C (400°F) Gas 6.

Start by making the pesto. Place the pine nuts in a dry frying pan/skillet and toast lightly over low-medium heat for a few minutes, shaking the pan regularly. Let cool, then put them in a food processor or blender with the rest of the pesto ingredients, and blitz until smooth. Set aside.

Rub a little olive oil onto the red/bell pepper and roast in the preheated oven until the skin blisters and turns black. Remove from oven, wrap in foil and, when cool enough, remove the skin. Slice into thin strips.

Brush the aubergine/eggplant and courgette/zucchini with olive oil and chargrill/broil on high for 2–3 minutes on each side. Do the same with the red onion, if using.

Divide the mozzarella ball into quarters. Then divide each quarter into 10 pieces.

Spread half a teaspoonful of pesto onto each crostini and top with the mozzarella and your choice of vegetables.

Season with a little pepper and serve.

This page: ajo blanco (p28), gazpacho (p28).
Opposite: mediterranean vegetable crostini
with pesto (p29), broad bean, ricotta & feta
crostini with pancetta (p29).

tortilla

The traditional way is to sauté the potatoes slowly in olive oil. I tend to cheat by zapping them in the microwave for a few minutes to speed things up.

2 onions, cubed

200 ml/scant 1 cup olive oil

600 g/1 lb. 5 oz. floury potatoes,
   peeled and cubed

10 eggs

3 pinches sea salt flakes

26-cm/10-in. non-stick, deep
frying pan/skillet

Makes 30

Start by caramelizing the onions in half of the olive oil for 15 minutes or so in the frying pan/skillet. Remove with a slotted spoon and set aside.

Meanwhile, microwave the potatoes in a plastic microwaveable bowl, with 2 tablespoons of water, for 3 minutes. Set aside.

Crack the eggs into a large bowl and beat with a fork. Do not whisk. Add the onions to the eggs.

Add the rest of the oil to the pan, add the potatoes and sauté for 5 minutes, turning often. Using a slotted spoon, transfer the fried potatoes from the oil into the egg mixture. Add the salt and mix together.

Pour all but 2 tablespoons of the olive oil out of the pan into a heatproof jug/pitcher and return the pan to the heat. Add the egg mixture to the pan and stir for 1 minute. As the tortilla begins to cook at the edges, pull the edges slowly into the middle, allowing the raw egg to take its place by tilting the pan. Cook for 6–10 minutes on a low heat.

When the base is cooked but the top is still wet, place a large plate on the top with one hand, and hold the pan with your other. Flip the tortilla over onto the plate and slide it back into the pan. Cook for 2 minutes more. Let cool. Slice into 3-cm/1¼-in. cubes (the corner pieces are the chef's perks).

butternut squash & chorizo skewers

600 g/21 oz. butternut squash

360 g/13 oz. chorizo

parsley leaves, to serve

For the marinade

2 tablespoons olive oil

2 pinches sea salt

a pinch of coarse black pepper

½ teaspoon ground fennel seeds

⅛ teaspoon ground cumin

baking sheet lined with a
silicone mat

Makes 35

Preheat the oven to 200°C (400°F) Gas 6.

Mix the ingredients for the marinade together in a bowl. Cut the butternut squash into 35 neat cubes, toss in the marinade and then transfer to the prepared baking sheet, making sure there is a little space between each cube of squash.

Cook in the preheated oven for 20 minutes or until the edges are crisp and the squash is cooked through.

Meanwhile, cut the chorizo into 35 pieces, heat a frying pan/skillet and fry the chorizo pieces for a couple of minutes on each side. Drain on paper towels.

Skewer through a parsley leaf, then the squash, then the chorizo. Serve.

paella 'arancini' & alioli

If there's not enough leftover paella to go around the whole family again the following day, I shape the cold rice into small balls, coat them in breadcrumbs and fry them for my own version of the Italian arancini. Top with a little alioli and parsley and you've got a very tasty canapé. If you don't have paella leftovers, this is how I make them from scratch.

1 tablespoon oil

1 onion

70 g/2½ oz. chorizo picante,
   finely diced

150 g/5½ oz. skinless boned
   chicken thighs, finely diced

2 garlic cloves, crushed

100 g/3½ oz. prawns/shrimp,
   finely diced

70 g/2 ½ oz. squid, finely diced

a pinch of saffron

1 tablespoon tomato purée/paste

600 ml/2½ cups chicken stock

300 g/generous 1½ cups
   paella rice

1 egg yolk

plain/all-purpose flour,
   for dusting

2 eggs, whisked, for egg-washing

200 g/scant 4 cups breadcrumbs

sunflower oil, for frying

freshly chopped parsley, to garnish

For the alioli

2 garlic cloves, crushed

100 g/½ cup mayonnaise

a pinch of paprika

a squeeze of lemon juice

Makes 40

Heat the oil in a large frying pan/skillet and sauté the onions, chorizo, chicken and garlic for 10 minutes.

Add the prawns/shrimp, squid, saffron, tomato purée/paste and stock, and bring to a simmer.

Add the rice and stir. Let simmer for 20 minutes and check the rice to see if it is tender. If it isn't, cook for a few minutes more. Take off the heat and let cool for 10 minutes, then mix in the egg yolk and spread on a tray to cool completely. Refrigerate for 2 hours.

Flour your hands and use a spoon to form the rice into balls a little smaller than a golf ball. Chill the rice balls again, until firm. When you are ready to cook, dust the rice balls in flour, dip in egg wash and finally in the breadcrumbs.

Heat the sunflower oil in a deep, heavy-bottomed saucepan until a breadcrumb sizzles in the oil. Fry the arancini, in batches, for 2–3 minutes, until the breadcrumbs are a deep golden brown and the centre is piping hot. Drain on paper towels and keep warm while you cook the rest. Serve.

To make the alioli, mix the crushed garlic cloves into the mayonnaise with the lemon juice and paprika.

To serve, cut each ball in half, top with alioli and sprinkle with chopped parsley.

Left to right: butternut squash & chorizo skewers (p32), tortilla (p32), paella 'arancini' & alioli (p33).

blinis

Adapted from a Delia Smith recipe. A squeezy bottle here really helps get even circles, but you can spoon them into the pan with two teaspoons for a more rustic look. You can prepare the blinis ahead and freeze them for up to 1 week.

40 g/⅓ cup spelt flour

130 g/generous 1 cup white strong/bread flour

1 teaspoon salt

1 x 7-g/¼-oz. sachet easy-blend/ rapid-rise dried yeast

150 ml/generous ½ cup crème fraîche/sour cream

175 ml/⅔ cup full-fat/whole milk

2 eggs, separated

30 g/2 tablespoons unsalted butter

a squeezy bottle

Makes approx 80 4-cm/1½-in. blinis

Sift together the flours and salt. Sprinkle over the yeast.

In a small saucepan, warm the crème fraîche/sour cream and the milk together. When it is warm to the touch (if it is too hot it will kill the yeast), whisk in the egg yolks. Pour the mixture over the flour and yeast. Mix well, cover with a kitchen towel and leave in a warm place for 1 hour.

In a clean bowl, whisk the egg whites until they form stiff peaks. With a large spoon, gently fold them into the batter. Spoon the batter into a squeezy bottle.

Heat a non-stick pan and, using a paper towel, rub butter all over the base. Squeeze out little 4-cm/1-½ in. blinis into the pan. Don't touch them until they are ready to turn. You will know they are ready when tiny bubbles appear through the batter. Use a palette knife to flip them over and cook briefly on the other side.

Cool on a wire rack, then serve. You can store them in the refrigerator or freeze, well wrapped. To serve, warm them in the oven 180°C (350°F) Gas 4 for 5–6 minutes. There is no need to defrost them first.

----

blue cheese, pear butter & walnut blinis

My American friend Nancy introduced me to 'apple butter' when she gave me a homemade jar of it. You wouldn't believe it has no sugar or butter in it; just slow-cooked fruits and spices. I have since made my own pear butter.

3 large ripe Williams/Comice pears, peeled, cored and diced

freshly squeezed juice of 1 lemon

100 g/3½ oz. blue cheese such as Stilton or Gorgonzola, crumbled

30 walnut halves

30 blinis (see above)

Makes 30

Put the pears in a non-stick pan and add the lemon juice.

Cook over a medium heat, stirring constantly for around 20 minutes, until you have a thick but loose paste.

Let the pear butter cool.

Top each blini with a little pear butter, blue cheese and a walnut half.

The pear butter will keep for 1 week stored in an airtight container in the refrigerator.

courgette & parmesan blinis

2 courgettes/zucchini
100 g/3½ oz. Parmesan
grated zest of ½ a lemon
1 garlic clove, crushed
1 tablespoon fresh thyme leaves
4 tablespoons olive oil
40 blinis (see opposite)
salt and freshly ground black pepper

Makes 40

Slice the courgettes/zucchini into 2-mm/¹⁄₁₆-in. slices. Using a vegetable peeler, peel 40 strips of Parmesan and place on top each blini. Set aside.

Heat a large ridged griddle pan over medium heat.

Meanwhile, mix the grated lemon zest, garlic and thyme leaves into the oil, season with salt and black pepper, and toss through the courgettes/zucchini.

Place the courgette/zucchini slices onto the hot griddle and cook for 1 minute, then flip over with tongs. When the edges start to crisp, transfer two pieces of courgette/zucchini onto each blini, then serve.

squash frittatas with pea purée & roasted tomatoes

250 g/½ lb butternut squash,
    peeled and finely diced
1 tablespoon olive oil
sprig of fresh rosemary or thyme
6 eggs
100 g/3½ oz. fresh spinach,
    finely chopped
100 g/3½ oz. feta cheese, crumbled
freshly ground black pepper

For the roast tomatoes
12 cherry tomatoes, halved
2 teaspoons olive oil
salt and freshly ground black
    pepper

For the pea purée
200 g/1½ cups frozen petits pois
1 teaspoon olive oil

baking sheet, lined with
baking parchment
24-hole mini muffin pan,
greased with a little olive oil
a squeezy bottle

Makes 24

The tomatoes can be made 1–2 days in advance. Preheat the oven to 180°C (350°F) Gas 4.

Slice the tomatoes in half. Place the halved tomatoes cut-side up on the prepared baking sheet, drizzle with the olive oil and season with salt and pepper. Cook in the preheated oven for 25–30 minutes, until shrivelled. Allow to cool then place in an airtight container and store at room temperature for up to 1 day, or in the refrigerator for up to 2 days.

For the pea purée, bring a saucepan of water to the boil and add the petits pois. Boil the petits pois for 2–3 minutes, then drain and refresh under cold running water. Place the petits pois into a food processor or blender with the olive oil and a pinch of salt, and blitz until smooth. Place in the refrigerator while you make the frittatas.

Preheat the oven to 200°C (400°F) Gas 6.

Put the butternut squash into a bowl with the olive oil and rosemary, and season with salt and pepper. Place in a roasting pan and bake in the preheated oven for 15 minutes, until the edges begin to crisp. Remove from the oven and lower the temperature to 180°C (350°F) Gas 4.

Beat the eggs in a large bowl with a fork and add the spinach. Add the crumbled feta and season with black pepper. Add the roasted squash, discarding the rosemary from the pan. Divide the mixture between the holes of the mini muffin pan, filling each hole to a little over half way. Place in the oven and cook for 10–11 minutes, until the egg has set.

Allow to cool in the pan for a few minutes, then lift the frittatas onto a wire rack to cool completely. Once cool, top each frittata with half a teaspoon of pea purée followed by a dried tomato. Serve.

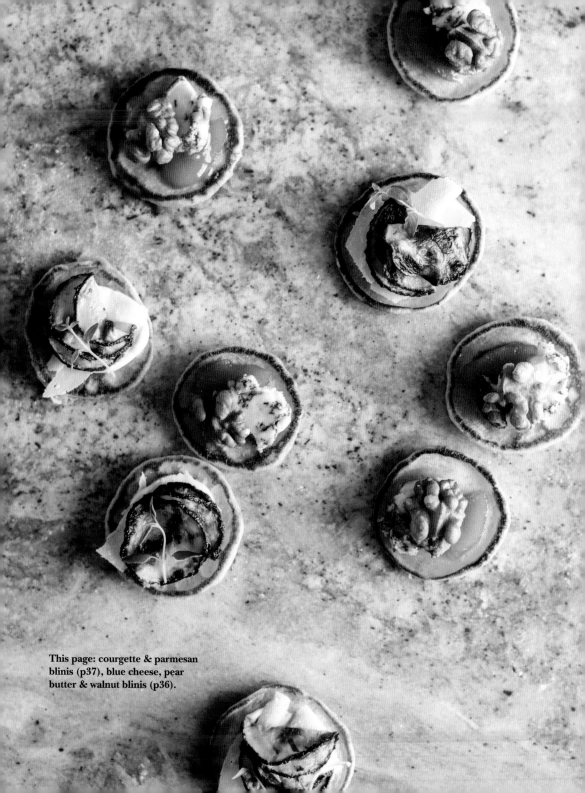

This page: courgette & parmesan
blinis (p37), blue cheese, pear
butter & walnut blinis (p36).

Top to bottom: prosciutto,
pear & gorgonzola rolls
(p41), squash frittatas
with pea purée & roasted
tomatoes (p37),
bocconcini skewers (p40).

bocconcini skewers

This is such a pretty canapé that it needs no decoration. Neither does it need any seasoning; the olive and sun-dried tomato adds all the saltiness it needs.

20 bocconcini (mini mozzarella balls)

20 fresh basil leaves

10 sun-dried tomatoes, halved

20 kalamata olives, pitted

mini plastic/wooden skewers

Makes 20

Wrap a basil leaf around a mozzarella ball and secure with a skewer.

Next push the sun-dried tomato and the olive up the skewer. Make sure there is only the tiniest bit of skewer showing at the end, so it is easy to eat. Serve.

artichoke, mozzarella & speck

15 chargrilled artichoke heart quarters from a jar

1 x 125-g/4½-oz ball of buffalo mozzarella

5 slices of speck or serrano ham (about 70 g/2½ oz)

15 small basil leaves

freshly ground black pepper

Makes 15

Cut each slice of speck crossways into three pieces, to make 15 pieces in total. Slice the mozzarella into 15 even pieces.

Drain the artichoke heart quarters in a sieve/strainer, then place them on paper towels to remove any excess oil.

Place a piece of speck on a board and put an artichoke quarter, a slice of mozzarella and a basil leaf on top. Sprinkle with ground black pepper, then roll the ham around the filling. Repeat with the remaining ingredients. Serve.

watermelon, feta, basil & balsamic

1 watermelon, cubed

100 g/3½ oz. feta cheese, cut into 40 pieces

40 small, fresh basil leaves

3 tablespoons balsamic reduction

Makes 40

Cut the watermelon into 2.5-cm/1-in. cubes and spoon out a little hole at the top of each cube (to allow space to stuff the cheese later). Turn upside down on paper towels and leave for 30 minutes in the refrigerator. Check after 15 minutes and replace the paper towels if they are wet through.

In the hole, place a piece of feta, a small basil leaf (upside down) and drop in a little balsamic reduction. Serve.

prosciutto, pear & gorgonzola rolls

5 slices prosciutto (about 70 g/2½ oz)

2 ripe pears, cored and each cut into 10 slices

200 g/7 oz. Gorgonzola, cut into 20 pieces

small handful of rocket/arugula

Makes 10

Cut the ham in half crossways, so you have 10 pieces.

Lay two pieces each of the pear, cheese and rocket/arugula inside both ends of the ham, with a little sticking out.

Roll tightly, cut in half down the middle and serve.

asparagus filo cigars

24 asparagus spears, trimmed to 10 cm/4 in.

180 g/6½ oz. filo/phyllo pastry (4 sheets of 47 x 28 cm/ 18½ x 11 in.)

2 x 150 g/5½ oz. packs of Boursin or other garlic and herb soft cheese

50 g/3 tablespoons unsalted butter, melted

Makes 24

Preheat the oven to 190°C (375°F) Gas 5.

Bring a pan of salted water to the boil and have a bowl of ice-cold water ready nearby. Drop the asparagus into the boiling water and lift out after 1½ minutes. Plunge into the cold water. Drain the asparagus and place on paper towels to dry.

Cut each sheet of filo/phyllo into a grid of 6 equal rectangles. At the short end of each rectangle, place the asparagus with the spear showing.

Cut the Boursin into 24 portions of cheese in total. Place a piece of cheese next to each asparagus spear.

Brush the filo/phyllo with a little of the melted butter and roll snugly into a cigar (do not roll too tightly or the pastry might burst).

Brush a little more butter on top of the pastry and bake in the oven, seal-side down, until golden and crisp: approximately 15–20 minutes. Remove from the oven, cool on a wire rack and serve.

scallops in pancetta

30 small scallops

15 pancetta slices, cut in half crossways

For the marinade

2 sprigs of fresh rosemary

5 fresh basil leaves

freshly squeezed juice and grated zest of ½ a lemon

2 tablespoons olive oil

salt and freshly ground black pepper

1 garlic clove, crushed

mini wooden skewers

Makes 30

Put the marinade ingredients together in a bowl.

Wrap each pancetta half around a scallop and skewer through the side. Spoon the marinade over, and marinate the scallops for 30–60 minutes.

Heat a frying pan/skillet and cook the scallops for just under 1 minute on each side. Then, for the last 10 seconds, add any leftover marinade to the pan. Serve.

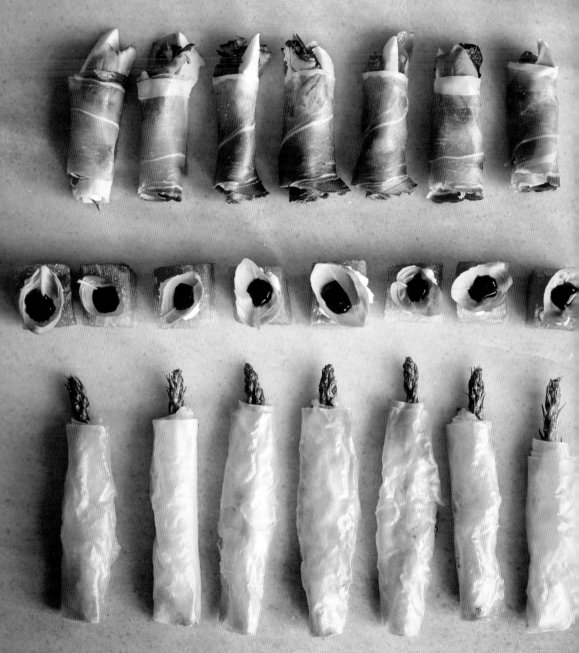

This page: artichoke, mozzarella & speck
(p40), watermelon, feta, basil & balsamic
(p40), asparagus filo cigars (p41).
Opposite: scallops in pancetta (p41).

crackers with cashew pâté, sun-dried tomatoes & dill

Thank you, Grace, for introducing me to the wonders of raw cashews.

240 g/2 cups raw cashews

1 tablespoon fresh chives,
chopped/snipped

1 tablespoon freshly chopped dill

½ tablespoon freshly chopped
rosemary

18 sun-dried tomatoes, halved

36 crackers, such as rye crackers

salt and freshly ground black pepper

a pinch of dill, to garnish

muslin/cheesecloth

Makes 36

Soak the cashews in water overnight.

Drain the cashews and whizz in a blender or food processor, with a little water if needed, until you have a paste.

Add most of the chopped herbs and season with salt and pepper. Place the cashew mix in muslin/cheesecloth and make a flattened ball/wheel. You can roll the wheel in more herbs if you like or use the herbs to sprinkle on the finished canapé. Tightly squeeze out any excess water and leave in the refrigerator until needed. (It will keep for a few days wrapped well in clingfilm/plastic wrap.)

To serve, top a cracker with a slice of the cashew pâté, followed by the sun-dried tomatoes and leftover herbs.

....

anise crackers, goat's cheese, honey & thyme

This is my take on the humble 'torta de aceite' from Andalucia.

120 g/1 cup
plain/all-purpose flour

½ teaspoon baking powder

½ teaspoon table salt

4 tablespoons water

3 tablespoons olive oil

2 teaspoons fennel or anise
seeds, crushed using a
pestle and mortar, plus
1 teaspoon to decorate

2 tablespoons
caster/granulated sugar,
to decorate

150 g/5½ oz. goat's cheese

honey, for drizzling

a few sprigs of fresh thyme

a baking sheet, lined with
baking parchment

a chef's blowtorch

Makes 40

Preheat the oven to 180°C (350°F) Gas 4.

Mix all the ingredients together to make a dough. Tip the dough out onto a floured surface and roll it until it is 2 mm/¹⁄₁₆ in. thick. Cut the dough into 5-cm/2-in. disks.

Put the disks onto the prepared baking sheet and cook in the preheated oven for 12 minutes.

Remove from the oven, sprinkle with caster/granulated sugar. Use the blowtorch to caramelize the surface.

Leave the crackers to cool on a wire rack.

Once the crackers are cool, spread with a little goat's cheese, drizzle with honey and place a thyme sprig on each. Serve.

crostini with truffled wild mushrooms

40 crostini (see page 28)

30 g/1 oz. dried porcini
  mushrooms

200 g/7 oz. baby chestnut
  mushrooms

100 g/3½ oz. chanterelle
  mushrooms

½ tablespoon unsalted
  butter

½ tablespoon olive oil

5 teaspoons truffle
  porcini paste

150 ml/generous ½ cup
  double/heavy cream

1 tablespoon freshly
  snipped chives

salt and freshly ground
  black pepper

Makes 40

First, make the crostini (see page 28). This step can be done a week before and the crostini kept in an airtight container.

Soak the porcini mushrooms in boiling water for at least 20 minutes. Meanwhile, slice the fresh mushrooms, and then slice the soaked porcini.

Heat the butter and olive oil in a frying pan/skillet over fairly high heat, and fry the mushrooms. After 10 minutes, add the truffled porcini and the cream. Reduce the cream a little, then season to taste.

Spread a teaspoon on each crostini and top with some chives. Serve.

leek & parmesan filo tartlets

2 tablespoons olive oil

400 g/14 oz. leeks, thinly
  sliced

150 ml/generous ½ cup
  double/ heavy cream

50 g/1¼ cup freshly grated
  Parmesan

25 filo/phyllo tartlet cases,
  (see page 90)

salt and freshly ground white
  pepper

Makes 25

Heat the olive oil in a frying pan/skillet and sauté the leeks for 5 minutes, until soft.

Add the cream and cook for 1 minute. Add the Parmesan, stir for 1 minute and turn off the heat. Season with white pepper and a touch of salt.

Fill the tartlet cases with a heaped teaspoon of the leek mixture and serve.

chestnuts & bacon

**The most eagerly anticipated dish of every party at my Auntie Sue's.
Don't be put off by the ingredients, you just have to trust me on this one!**

30 cooked, canned chestnuts

10 rashers/strips of bacon,
  each cut into 3 pieces

For the sauce

90 g/½ cup brown sugar

115 ml/½ cup mayonnaise

1 tablespoon sriracha
  chilli/hot pepper sauce

60 ml/¼ cup sweet chilli sauce

2 tablespoons soy sauce

a baking sheet, lined with
baking parchment

30 wooden skewers

Makes 30

Preheat the oven to 190°C (375°F) Gas 5.

Wrap a chestnut in 1 strip of bacon and secure with a toothpick/cocktail stick. Place on the prepared baking sheet.

Mix the sauce ingredients together and drizzle over the chestnuts. Bake in the preheated oven for 20 minutes.

Remove from the oven, cool slightly and serve.

Scandinavian

Food from Sweden, Norway and Denmark lends itself to pretty canapés, with beautiful open sandwiches and smörgåsbords of delightful crackers and nibbles. The clean, fresh flavours are perfect for summer entertaining.

smoked mackerel, apple & fennel on rye

Here is a canapé topping that can be made a few days in advance. Just keep the pâté in an airtight container in the refrigerator, until needed.

200 g/7 oz. boneless smoked
    mackerel fillets
20 g/1 generous tablespoon
    unsalted butter, softened
1 teaspoon Dijon mustard
1 generous tablespoon
    freshly grated horseradish
5 tablespoons crème fraîche/
    sour cream
freshly squeezed juice of
    ½ a lemon

1 teaspoon freshly
    chopped/snipped dill
freshly ground black pepper
35 mini rye crispbreads
1 apple, thinly sliced
½ fennel, thinly sliced

Makes 35

Discard the skin from the mackerel fillets, then flake them into a food processor.

Add the butter, mustard, horseradish, crème fraîche/sour cream, lemon juice, dill and some black pepper, then blend until smooth.

Spread a heaped teaspoonful of the mackerel pâté onto each crispbread and top with thinly sliced apple and fennel. Serve.

---

beetroot, cucumber & apple on crispbread

You can see by the length of this recipe how quick it is to prepare. We're spoilt for choice for gourmet crackers now, so take your pick and mix it up.

½ Gala apple, diced
8-cm/3-in. stick of
    cucumber, deseeded
    and diced
1 pickled beetroot/beet
    (about 60 g/2 oz.), diced
¼ red onion, diced
2 thumb-sized
    cornichons, diced
4 tablespoons crème
    fraîche/sour cream

1 teaspoon Dijon mustard
a squeeze of fresh lemon
    juice
a pinch of salt
35 crispbreads/crackers
    of your choice
dill, to garnish

Makes 35

Put the diced apple, cucumber, beetroot/beet, onion and cornichons into a bowl. Add the crème fraîche/sour cream, mustard, lemon and salt, and mix until combined. Taste to check the seasoning, and add more salt if needed.

Spoon a little of the mixture onto each crispbread or cracker and garnish with some dill. Serve.

rare roast beef & remoulade on rye

When Central London makes me weary, I pop into my favourite Scandinavian café, ScandiKitchen, for a pick-me-up in the form of a strong coffee and an open sandwich. These canapés are a take on just that. Roast beef and remoulade is a classic combination that's too pretty to be concealed. Alternatively, serve on crostini.

300 g/10½ oz. beef fillet/
   tenderloin
1 tablespoon olive oil
5 slices rye bread

For the remoulade
150 g/5 oz. celeriac, cut into
   2.5-cm/1-in. matchsticks
freshly squeezed juice of ½ lemon
1 tablespoon mayonnaise
1 teaspoon Dijon mustard
1 tablespoon crème fraîche/
   sour cream
1 tablespoon freshly chopped
   flat-leaf parsley
salt and freshly ground
   white pepper

Makes 30

Cut the beef fillet/tenderloin in half lengthways. Oil, season and massage well.

In a hot, dry pan, sear the beef for a few minutes on each side, wrap in foil and leave to rest for at least 20 minutes before carving. That way the meat relaxes and the juices are absorbed into the meat. Once the meat is cool, you can refrigerate it, covered, until you are ready to assemble the canapés.

To make the remoulade, combine the celeriac/celery root, lemon juice, mayonnaise, mustard, crème fraîche/sour cream and parsley, and season to taste with salt and pepper.

Thinly slice the beef across the grain into 30 pieces.

Take the rye bread and cut each slice into 6 square pieces. Top the rye bread with a slice of beef and some remoulade. Serve.

Smoked mackerel, apple & fennel on rye
(p50), beetroot, cucumber & apple on
crispbread (p50), rare roast beef &
remoulade on rye (p51).

beetroot salmon blinis

I love the vibrant fuchsia of the salmon next to the pop of black caviar on these blinis. Curing a side of fresh salmon in beetroot and gin is a tasty way to cater for a large number. However, here I show you a quick cheat, using smoked salmon and pickled beetroot juice.

4 tablespoons pickled beetroot/
   beet juice
2 teaspoons gin
100 g/3½ oz. smoked salmon
30 blinis (see recipe, page 36)
100 ml/scant ½ cup crème
   fraîche/sour cream
freshly squeezed juice of
   1 lemon
50 g/2 oz. lumpfish caviar

Makes 30

Pour the pickled beetroot/beet juice into a small container or shallow bowl. Add the gin and the salmon and leave for 5 minutes. (Alternatively, use store-bought beetroot-/beet-cured salmon.)

Slice the salmon into 30 pieces. Top each blini with ½ teaspoon of crème fraîche/sour cream, a piece of salmon, a squeeze of lemon and a little caviar. Serve.

....

quail's egg, crayfish & caviar blinis

A quail's egg always seems like a treat as most of us don't eat them regularly at home, so they make these blinis elegant and rich. You can use either chives or dill here. The salmon caviar adds a lovely deep saltiness, so if you are not using it, make sure to season the egg well.

8 quail's eggs
30 blinis (see recipe on page 36)
100 ml/scant ½ cup crème
   fraîche/sour cream
60 g/2 oz. crayfish tails
50 g/1½ oz. salmon caviar
1 tablespoon freshly chopped/
   snipped chives, to garnish

Makes 30

First, soft-boil the quail's eggs. Fill a small saucepan two-thirds full with water and bring it to the boil. Use a slotted spoon to lower the eggs gently into the water. After 2 minutes, remove and plunge the eggs straight into a bowl of cold water.

Once cool, tap each egg on the counter and gently roll to crack the shell. Carefully peel off the shells and rinse each egg in cold water. Slice each egg into quarters, lengthways.

Top each blini with ½ teaspoon of crème fraiche/sour cream, a crayfish tail and a quail-egg quarter.

Carefully top with a little salmon caviar and sprinkle on some chives.

cream cheese puffs with smoked salmon

50 ml/3½ tablespoons full-fat/
  whole milk
45 g/3 tablespoons unsalted butter
1 teaspoon caster/granulated sugar
80 g/⅔ cup plain/all-purpose flour
3 eggs, beaten
350 g/¾ lb. cream cheese
2 tablespoons freshly chopped dill,
  plus extra fronds to garnish
zest and juice of 1 lemon
salt and freshly ground black pepper
100 g/3½ oz. smoked salmon or
  salmon caviar

a baking sheet, lined with
baking parchment

Makes 30

Preheat the oven to 200°C (400°F) Gas 6.

Bring the milk, butter, sugar, a pinch of salt and 50 ml/3½ tablespoons water to the boil in a saucepan, then turn the heat to its lowest setting. Tip in the flour and, with a wooden spoon, beat until it forms a ball. Keep cooking on low heat for 2 minutes, moving the dough around the pan. Remove from the heat and let cool for 5 minutes.

Add the eggs, a little at a time, beating until the dough is a dropping consistency. Transfer to a piping/pastry bag and let rest for 5–10 minutes. Pipe 30 small shells onto the baking sheet, spacing them 2.5 cm/1 in. apart. Bake for 10 minutes, then increase the heat to 220°C (425°F) Gas 7 and cook for 5 minutes more. Transfer to a wire rack and poke holes in the top of each puff to let steam escape. Let cool completely.

Mix the cream cheese and dill in a bowl. Add half the lemon zest and juice, and season with pepper. Slice the tops off the puffs with a serrated knife and fill with a teaspoon of cream cheese. Top with smoked salmon or caviar. Garnish with dill fronds and serve.

seared beef fillet with horseradish

350 g/12½ oz. beef fillet/tenderloin
1 tablespoon olive oil
2 tablespoons freshly grated
  horseradish (or from a jar)
100 ml/scant ½ cup crème
  fraîche/sour cream
3 sprigs fresh rosemary
salt

30 mini wooden skewers

Makes 30

Cut the beef fillet/tenderloin in half lengthways. Oil, season and massage well.

In a hot, dry pan, sear the beef for a few minutes on each side, wrap in foil and leave to rest for at least 20 minutes before carving. That way the meat relaxes and the juices are absorbed into the meat.

Cut the meat across the grain into 30 strips and put each one on a mini skewer.

Mix the horseradish with the crème fraîche/sour cream and a pinch of salt. Garnish with the horseradish sauce and a few rosemary leaves, and serve.

beetroot, dill & goat's cheese cups

1 x 400-g/14-oz. can of
  chickpeas, drained
250 g/9 oz. cooked
  beetroot/beets
1 large garlic clove
2 tablespoons olive oil
1 tablespoon lemon juice

1½ tablespoons tahini
2–3 large pinches of salt
160 g/5½ oz. soft goat's cheese
fresh dill, to garnish
40 store-bought canapé cups

Makes 40

Put the drained chickpeas, cooked beetroot/ beets, garlic, olive oil, lemon juice, tahini and salt in a food processor, and blend until smooth.

Place a teaspoonful of the mixture in each canapé cup, and top with ½ teaspoon goat's cheese. Garnish with dill, and serve.

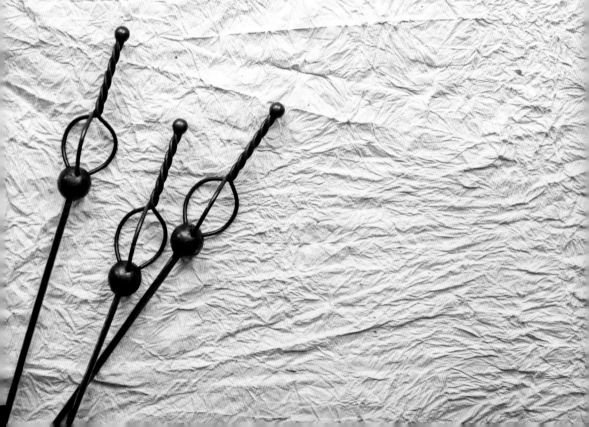

Indian

Indian spices lend themselves to nibbles, as a small bite can really pack a punch. I urge you to try the Pani Puri, a popular street food snack that will really give your friends an unexpected taste experience.

spicy salmon skewers

500 g/18 oz. salmon fillet
1 red onion, cut into
    2-cm/1-in. squares
    (optional)
freshly squeezed lemon juice,
    to serve
fresh coriander/cilantro,
    to garnish (optional)

For the marinade
100 ml/⅓ cup vegetable oil,
    plus extra for frying
2 heaped teaspoons grated
    fresh ginger

3 garlic cloves, grated
2–3 medium fresh red
    chillies/chiles, finely
    chopped
½ teaspoon each chilli/chili
    powder and garam
    masala
2 pinches of salt

25 small wooden skewers

Makes about 25

Discard the skin from the salmon fillet, then cut it into about 50 2-cm/1-in. cubes.

Mix the marinade ingredients together in a bowl, then add the salmon cubes and leave to marinate for at least 2 hours or overnight, covered, in the refrigerator.

Skewer the salmon cubes onto small wooden skewers, separated by onion slices, if you wish. Two cubes is ideal, but you can put one or three cubes on each stick, if you prefer.

Heat a little vegetable oil in a ridged griddle pan or frying pan/skillet. Fry the salmon, in batches, turning regularly, until cooked through. Squeeze the lemon over and garnish with fresh coriander/cilantro, if you like. Serve.

chicken tikka skewers

300 g/10½ oz. boneless,
    skinless chicken thighs
vegetable oil, for frying
freshly squeezed lemon or
    lime juice, to serve
fresh coriander/cilantro,
    to garnish (optional)

For the marinade
1 garlic clove, crushed
1 teaspoon grated
    fresh ginger
freshly squeezed juice
    of ½ a lemon
¼ teaspoon freshly ground
    black pepper

3 tablespoons natural/
    plain yogurt
⅛ teaspoon chilli/chili
    powder
1 cardamom pod
⅛ teaspoon ground
    cinnamon
½ teaspoon ground cumin
¼ teaspoon ground
    coriander

30 small wooden skewers

Makes 30

Cut the chicken into 30 pieces.

Mix the marinade ingredients together in a bowl, then add the chicken and leave to marinate, covered, overnight in the refrigerator.

Bring the chicken to room temperature. Skewer the chicken onto small wooden skewers. Heat a little vegetable oil in a ridged griddle pan or frying pan/skillet. Cook the chicken for 5–7 minutes, turning regularly, until cooked through.

Squeeze over some lemon or lime juice to taste and garnish with fresh coriander/cilantro, if you wish. Serve.

onion bhajis

2 onions, thinly sliced

2 large pinches of salt

2 garlic cloves, crushed

thumb-sized piece of fresh
  ginger, grated

1½ teaspoons ground cumin

½ teaspoon fennel seeds,
  crushed

½ teaspoon turmeric

2 fresh green chillies/chiles,
  finely chopped

½ teaspoon chilli/chili
  powder

4 fresh curry leaves
  (optional, but don't used
  dried ones)

2 tablespoons natural/plain
  yogurt

½ small bunch of fresh
  coriander/cilantro,
  chopped

100 g/3½ oz. gram/
  chickpea flour

Makes 35–40

Put the onions into a large bowl. Sprinkle on the salt and squeeze the onion slices with your hands to extract the juices.

Add the remaining ingredients and stir. Taste and season accordingly. If the batter is too doughy, add a little cold water to the mix.

In a large frying pan/skillet, heat the sunflower oil to 180°C (350°F). Test-fry a bhaji by dropping a teaspoonful of the mixture into the oil.
It should take only a couple of minutes to cook.

Continue to fry all the bhajis in the same way, drain on paper towels and serve.

pani puri

1 large potato, peeled, cut
  into 1-cm/½-in. cubes
  and boiled for 10 minutes

vegetable oil, for deep-frying

Pani (spicy water)

30 g/1 cup fresh mint leaves

10 g/⅓ cup fresh coriander/
  cilantro leaves

2 large green chillies, chopped

1 tablespoon tamarind
  concentrate or
  3 tablespoons
  tamarind pulp

freshly squeezed juice of
  ½ a large lemon

2 teaspoons salt

½ teaspoon fresh ginger,
  chopped/grated

2 tablespoons ground cumin

1 tablespoon caster/
  granulated sugar

Puri (semolina shell)

65 g/scant ½ cup semolina

20 g/2⅓ tablespoons
  plain/all-purpose flour

a pinch of salt

Makes 30–40

To make the pani, put all of the ingredients in a food processor or blender with 700 ml/3 cups water. Blend well, then strain. Set the pani water aside.

To make the puri, mix the semolina, flour and salt in a bowl and add 30 ml/⅛ cup water. Mix with your hands and add more water until it comes together. You should need no more than 60 ml/¼ cup water in total. Knead the dough for 5 minutes until soft. Cover with a damp kitchen towel for 10 minutes.

Heat the oil for deep-frying in a deep pan to 180°C (350°F). Pinch little balls (the size of a plump chickpea) from the dough and roll them into very thin flat disks.

Drop them into the oil in batches. They will sink to the bottom and, in seconds, rise to the top. With a slotted spoon, press them under the oil to puff up. Turn them over so that they brown on both sides. Drain on paper towels. Once cooled, tap a hole into the top of each puri, drop a couple of potato cubes in and a tablespoon of pani water. Serve immediately.

Overleaf, clockwise from left: pani puri (p61), onion bhajis (p61), chicken tikka skewers (p60), spicy salmon skewers (p60).

spinach, fennel & cumin ricotta cakes

This recipe is inspired by Deena, who creates the most mouthwatering vegetarian recipes.

80 g/3 oz. fresh spinach
½ teaspoon cumin seeds
1½ teaspoons fennel seeds
1 tablespoon vegetable oil
180 g/6½ oz. ricotta, plus extra to serve
70 g/generous ½ cup plain/ all-purpose flour
1 teaspoon baking powder
2 eggs, separated
100 ml/scant ½ cup whole milk
2 pinches of salt
vegetable oil, for frying
chopped spring onions/scallions, to garnish

Makes 40

Shred the spinach leaves in a food processor.

In a small frying pan/skillet, warm the cumin and fennel seeds in the oil, but don't let the seeds pop/toast, or they will taste bitter.

Add the seeds, ricotta, flour, baking powder, egg yolks and milk to the food processor and season.

Whizz until combined and transfer to a large bowl.

Whisk the egg whites until stiff and fold them into the spinach mixture.

Heat 2 tablespoons vegetable oil in a large frying pan/skillet over a high heat and drop heaped teaspoons of the mixture into the oil. Fry for about 30 seconds on each side, or until cooked through. Continue to cook the remaining mixture, adding extra oil to the pan, if needed.

These are delicious served just as they are, or you can spoon a little extra ricotta on top and sprinkle with chopped spring onions/scallions.

tandoori prawns with minty yogurt dip

20 king prawns/jumbo shrimp, shelled and deveined
1 tablespoon sunflower oil
1 tablespoon unsalted butter

For the marinade
2 tablespoons sunflower oil
freshly squeezed juice of 1 lime
1 fresh green or red chilli/chile
2 garlic cloves
thumb-sized piece of fresh ginger, grated
1 teaspoon garam masala

2 teaspoons ground cumin
½ teaspoon turmeric
½ teaspoon white pepper
a pinch of salt
3 tablespoons natural/ plain yogurt

For the minty yogurt dip
150 ml/⅔ cup natural/ plain yogurt
2 tablespoons freshly chopped mint
1 garlic clove, crushed
a pinch of salt

Makes 20

For the minty yogurt dip, mix the ingredients together. Chill until ready to serve.

To make the marinade, blitz all the ingredients together in a food processor.

In a large bowl, marinate the prawns/shrimp for 2 hours.

Heat a frying pan/skillet, add the oil, followed by the butter.

Use a slotted spoon to drop the prawns/shrimp into the frying pan/skillet and fry on a high heat for 1 minute on each side in 2 batches.

Serve the prawns/shrimp with the dip.

spiced coconut lamb skewers

This is a great 'make ahead' canapé as you can have the lamb skewered and
marinating in the refrigerator overnight, ready to grill minutes before serving.

500 g/1 lb. 2 oz. boned
   lamb shoulder or leg
   meat, cut across the grain
   into 45 bite-sized strips
   (approx. 10 g/¼ oz. each)
vegetable oil, for brushing
chilli/chili powder, for
   sprinkling (optional)
freshly squeezed lemon juice,
   to serve
sea salt flakes, to serve

For the marinade
2 garlic cloves, crushed
thumb-sized piece of fresh
   ginger, grated
2 teaspoons ground coriander
1 teaspoon ground cumin
2 pinches of salt
1 teaspoon chilli/chili powder
200 ml/scant 1 cup coconut
   milk

Makes 45

To make the marinade, combine all the ingredients
except the coconut milk and rub it into the strips
of lamb. Mix in the coconut milk and refrigerate
for at least 1 hour or overnight.

You can skewer the lamb before or after marinating
but you save on refrigerator space by doing it after.

Brush a very hot griddle pan with vegetable oil and
cook the skewers for 40–60 seconds on each side,
or until cooked to your liking.

Sprinkle with sea salt flakes, squeeze over some
lemon juice and sprinkle with chilli/chili powder,
if you wish.

pea & potato samosas

300 g/10½ oz. potato, diced
a pinch of salt
2–3 tablespoons vegetable oil
2 shallots, finely sliced
2 garlic cloves, crushed
thumb-sized piece of fresh ginger,
   grated
1 teaspoon unsalted butter
100 g/scant 1 cup frozen petits pois
1 small fresh green chilli/chile,
   finely chopped (optional)
½ teaspoon toasted cumin seeds
1 tablespoon freshly chopped
   coriander/cilantro
salt and freshly ground black pepper
270 g/9½ oz. filo/phyllo pastry
vegetable oil, for frying
mango chutney, to serve (optional)

Makes 40

Put the potato in a large pan, cover with cold water, add the salt and
bring to the boil. Simmer for approximately 8–10 minutes or until soft.
Drain and mash lightly.

Heat the oil in a frying pan/skillet, add the shallots and cook for about
5 minutes, until softened. Add the garlic, ginger and butter to the
shallots and fry for another minute. Add to the potato.

Cook the peas, then add them to the potato mixture along with the
chilli/chile, if using, cumin seeds and chopped coriander/cilantro.
Season to taste.

Cut the filo/phyllo pastry into 23 x 6-cm/9 x 2½-in. strips and put a
teaspoonful of the potato mix in the left corner. Fold the pastry over
into a triangle until the samosa is sealed. Dab on a little oil to stick the
last fold in place.

Shallow-fry the samosas for a minute or so on each side until the pastry
is crisp. Drain on paper towels.

Serve with mango chutney, if desired.

Clockwise from bottom left: spinach, fennel & cumin ricotta cakes (p64), spiced coconut lamb skewers (p65), tandoori prawns with minty yogurt dip (p64), pea & potato samosas (p65).

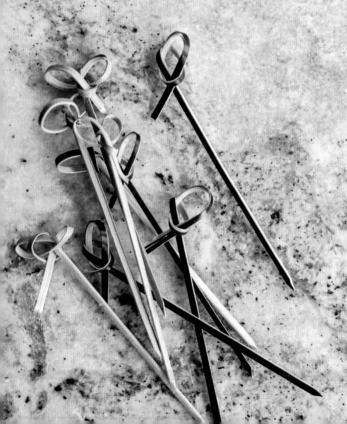

Asian

These Asian-inspired recipes will add a little elegance to your party. If using raw fish puts you off the idea of making sushi, try the easy alternative fillings in this chapter from my friend Reiko. There are plenty of sumptuous meat and vegetable canapés here too.

sushi rice

*350 g/scant 2 cups white
short-grain rice, such as
sushi rice*
100 ml/⅓ cup sushi vinegar

Makes 700–800 g/25–28 oz.

Place the rice in a sieve/strainer and lower into a large bowl of water. Wash the rice in the water with your hands until the water turns milky. Repeat with fresh water, until the water stays clear. Put the rice in a large saucepan, cover with 385 ml/1⅔ cups water and leave for 30 minutes.

Cover the pan with a lid (ideally a lid with a little hole in it to release steam). Bring to the boil over medium-high heat. Listen carefully to the water – as soon as it comes to the boil, turn the heat down to the lowest setting and leave to cook for 15 minutes, without lifting the lid. Remove from the heat and leave for 10–15 minutes to steam with the lid on.

Tip the hot rice into a large wooden bowl. Gradually pour in the vinegar, folding it into the rice using a slicing action to coat the grains and separate them. Do not stir or you will squash the rice. While you fold the rice, fan it with the other hand to bring it to room temperature. It should be shiny and sticky. Cover with a damp kitchen towel until ready to use.

pickled mackerel compressed sushi

a few pinches of fine table salt
2 mackerel fillets
150 ml/⅔ cup sushi vinegar
*1 tablespoon pickled ginger,
chopped*
*½ quantity prepared sushi rice
(see above)*

a shallow plastic container,
about 17 x 11 cm/6½ x 4¼ in.
in size

Makes 35

Sprinkle the salt over both sides of the mackerel and leave for 15 minutes. Brush off most of the salt with paper towels and pat the fillets dry.

Trim the fillets to the length of the container and keep the trimmings. Place all the mackerel in the container and pour over the sushi vinegar. Cover and place in the refrigerator for 2 hours, then turn the fillets. You can leave the mackerel overnight, if you like, but it should be ready after a further 2 hours. Remove the mackerel, pat dry and carefully peel off the thin film that will have developed over the skin.

Clean and dry the container, then line it with clingfilm/plastic wrap, leaving plenty draped over the edge.

Wet your hands and place 2 cm/¾ in. of rice into the bottom of the container. Gently press it down to compact it and level the top. Sprinkle over the pickled ginger and then press the mackerel fillets, side by side, flesh-side down on top. Use the trimmings to fill any gaps.

Gather the overhanging clingfilm/plastic and lay it over the mackerel. Find a lid or board that will sit just inside of the container and place this on top, then lay some heavy books on top. Leave for 2 hours in a cool room (not in the refrigerator).

Carefully lift out the compressed sushi and slice lengthways into 3 strips, then into 5 strips across to make 15 squares. Serve with soy sauce.

honey soy mackerel & daikon maki

¼ quantity prepared sushi rice
(see left)

1½ sheets nori seaweed

3 pea-sized drops of wasabi
paste

3 x 1-cm/½-inch strips pickled
daikon radish

1 fillet smoked honey soy
mackerel (approx 80 g/3 oz.)

a sushi mat

Makes 18–21

Fold the whole nori sheet in half across the grain and carefully tear in two. Lay the nori, shiny-side down, on a sushi mat.

Wet your hands slightly. Take one-third of the rice and spread it evenly over the nori. Leave 1 cm/½ in. free of rice along the top edge.

Gently press the rice down and spread a pea-sized drop of wasabi paste across the length of the rice. Line one strip of daikon along the middle of the rice and one-third of the mackerel next to it. Bring the bottom edge of the mat up and roll so that the top edge of the nori meets the edge of the rice. Apply gentle pressure so that the roll is tight and the margin of nori will overlap. Put the roll to one side with the overlap at the base. The moisture present in the rice will stick the nori together.

Repeat with the other 2 nori sheets and the remaining ingredients, keeping the finished roll covered. Slice each roll into 6 (or 7 if you like the look of filling coming out of the end, as pictured overleaf).

crabstick & avocado maki

¼ quantity prepared sushi rice
(see left)

1½ sheets nori seaweed

3 pea-sized drops of wasabi
paste

1 just-ripe avocado, halved
and stone/pit removed

120 g/4 oz. good-quality
crabsticks, sliced into thin
strips (or cooked prawns/
shrimp)

Makes 18–21

Fold the whole nori sheet in half across the grain and carefully tear in two. Lay the nori, shiny-side down, on a sushi mat (or folded kitchen towel).

Wet your hands slightly. Take one-third of the rice and spread it evenly over the nori. Leave 1 cm/½ in. free of rice along the top edge.

Gently press the rice down and spread a pea-sized drop of wasabi paste across the length of the rice. Slice the avocado into thin strips. Line one-third of the avocado strips along the middle of the rice and one-third of the crabsticks next to it. Bring the bottom edge of the mat up and roll so that the top edge of the nori meets the edge of the rice. Apply gentle pressure so that the roll is tight and the margin of nori will overlap.

Put the roll to one side with the overlap at the base. The moisture present in the rice will stick the nori together.

Repeat with the other 2 nori sheets and the remaining ingredients, keeping the finished roll covered. Slice each roll into 6 (or 7 if you like the look of filling coming out of the end, as pictured overleaf).

**Overleaf from left to right: honey soy mackerel &
daikon maki (p71), crabstick & avocado maki (p71),
pickled mackerel compressed sushi (p70).**

smoked salmon, enoki & white miso cucumber boats

I always welcome light bites like this, served as a refreshing palate cleanser amidst heavier or richer canapés. Make sure the enoki are very fresh and clean.

2 x 200-g/7-oz. cucumbers,
    cut in half and deseeded
200 g/7 oz. smoked salmon
4 tablespoons white miso paste
100 g/3½ oz. enoki mushrooms
60 g/2 oz. sliced pickled ginger
1 tablespoon black or white
    sesame seeds, to garnish
    (optional)

Makes 40

Take each cucumber half and peel a strip of skin from the rounded side so that it will sit flat on the work surface. Slice the cucumber at a right angle into 2-cm/¾-in. wide strips.

Cut the salmon into 40 pieces (5 g/⅛ oz. each) and place a piece on each slice of cucumber.

Spoon a pea-sized amount of white miso paste on the base of each piece of salmon.

Cut the top 4 cm/1½ in. off the enoki mushrooms and place a few at a time on each of the dots of miso.

Top with a little pickled ginger and serve sprinkled with a pinch of sesame seeds, if using.

tofu, ginger & lime spoons

With refreshing, delicate flavours, this canape is the perfect accompaniment to a glass of fizz to kick off a summer party. I love the light zing of a lime or a splash of yuzu, but you can substitute with a little soy or tamari if you'd like something richer. You can use silken tofu, the most important thing is that it is fresh and great quality. The best kind to go for is the tofu you find stored in a tub of water in Asian supermarkets.

500 g/1 lb. 2 oz. fresh, firm tofu
90 g/3 oz. grated fresh ginger
2 spring onions/scallions,
    thinly sliced
freshly squeezed lime juice,
    to serve

32 canapé spoons

Makes 32

Place the tofu on a few layers of paper towels to absorb the excess liquid. Slice the tofu into small cubes that fit nicely onto your spoons (roughly 2.5 x 3 cm/1 x 1¼ in.).

Place a piece of tofu on each spoon and gently place a pinch of grated ginger on top. Place a pinch of the spring onions/scallions on top of the ginger and, just before serving, sprinkle a little lime juice over each spoon.

sesame prawn toasts

10 slices (slightly stale) white
  bread, crusts removed
30–40 coriander/cilantro
  leaves to garnish
5 tablespoons sesame seeds
400 ml/1¼ cups groundnut/
  peanut or vegetable oil
plum or sweet chilli/chili
  sauce, to serve

For the topping
6 spring onions/scallions,
  roughly chopped
450 g/1 lb. raw prawns/

shrimp, peeled and deveined
1 teaspoon freshly chopped
  coriander/cilantro
1 garlic clove, crushed
1 tablespoon grated
  fresh ginger
1 egg white
2 teaspoons soy sauce
1 tablespoon cornflour/
  cornstarch

Makes 30

To make the topping, whizz the spring onions/
scallions in a food processor. Add the rest of the
ingredients and whizz again.

Spread the topping onto each slice of bread.
Sprinkle the sesame seeds on a plate and gently
press each slice of bread, prawn-/shrimp-side
down, into the seeds. Cut each slice into 3 fingers
and press a coriander/cilantro leaf into one end.

Heat the oil in frying pan/skillet. Cook the toast
topping-side down for a couple of minutes. Flip over
and cook for 40 seconds more, until crisp. Drain
on paper towels. Serve with plum or sweet chilli/
chili sauce.

crushed yellow bean prawns

2 tablespoons vegetable oil
3 garlic cloves, finely chopped
1 fresh red chilli/chile,
  deseeded and finely
  chopped
2.5-cm/1-in. piece of fresh
  ginger, grated
20 raw king prawns/jumbo
  shrimp, peeled and
  deveined, with tails left on

3 tablespoons yellow
  bean sauce
1 tablespoon Shaoxing rice
  wine or dry sherry
1 tablespoon caster/
  granulated sugar
1 fresh red chilli/chile,
  sliced, to garnish

Makes 20

Heat the oil in a wok or large frying pan/skillet over
high heat. Add the garlic, chilli/chile and ginger.
After 10 seconds, add the prawns/shrimp and toss
to combine.

Then add the yellow bean sauce, Shaoxing wine,
1 tablespoon water and the sugar.

After 4 minutes, check a prawn/shrimp to see if it is
cooked. Scatter with fresh chilli/chile and serve.

chilli devilled eggs

12 hard-boiled/hard-cooked
  eggs, peeled
4 tablespoons mayonnaise
1–2 tablespoons chilli/chili
  shrimp paste
salt and ground white
  pepper

2 spring onions/scallions
1 teaspoon black sesame
  seeds, to serve

Makes 24

Halve the eggs lengthways and remove the yolks. Put
the yolks into a bowl and break them up with a fork.

Mix in the mayonnaise and chilli/chili shrimp
paste to taste. Season with salt and white pepper.
When smooth, either spoon back into the eggs or
pipe with a star-shaped nozzle, if you have one.

Sprinkle over the sliced spring onions/scallions
and black sesame seeds and serve.

duck breast chinese pancakes
with ginger jammy plums

You could roast a duck if you want it crispy, but it will take a couple of hours.
I prefer to cook the breast to save on roasting and shredding time – it's juicy
and easy to portion. The ginger jammy plums is something I do, not only to
add flavour, but because I think they look gorgeous.

175 g/6 oz. duck breast
10 ready-made Chinese
  pancakes (about 14 cm/
  5½ in. in diameter)
2 Chinese teaspoons five spice
  mixed with ½ teaspoon salt

For the jammy plums
2 plums cut into 20 wedges
freshly squeezed juice of
  1 orange
1 teaspoon grated fresh ginger
1 teaspoon caster/granulated
  sugar

10 teaspoons hoisin sauce
½ a cucumber, cut into
  matchsticks
5 spring onions/scallions,
  cut into matchsticks

Makes 20

To make the jammy plums, simmer the plums in the orange juice,
ginger and sugar for 3 minutes in a shallow frying pan/skillet until they
take on a jam-like texture.

Take the duck out of the fridge 20 minutes before cooking. Score the
skin of the duck and trim off any excess fat around the sides.

Rub the five spice and salt mix all over the duck. Put it in a frying
pan/skillet skin-side down and turn on the heat.

When the pan is hot and you can hear the duck start to sizzle, let it cook
for 5 minutes.

Sear the duck on the sides and the bottom, cooking for a further
5–8 minutes, or until cooked to your liking.

Take the pan off the heat and leave the duck to rest.

Lay the pancakes flat on a chopping board and cut in half.

Spoon ½ teaspoon hoisin sauce on a half-pancake and arrange a piece
of duck, a wedge of jammy plum and a few matchsticks of cucumber and
spring onions/scallions on top. Tightly roll into a flat cone. Repeat with
the remaining ingredients and serve.

crab, mango & avocado rolls

½ a ripe mango

1 ripe hass avocado

3 spring onions/scallions,
  finely chopped

2 teaspoons freshly chopped
  coriander/cilantro

100 g/3½ oz. white crabmeat

freshly squeezed juice of ¼ of
  a lime

2 teaspoons mayonnaise

½ a medium fresh red
  chilli/chile, finely chopped

Tabasco, to taste

8 x 18 cm/7 in. rice papers

Makes 16

Cut the mango and avocado into thin strips.

In a bowl, mix together the spring onions/scallions, chopped coriander/cilantro, crab, lime juice, mayonnaise and chilli/chile. Add Tabasco to taste.

Lay out a clean kitchen towel. One by one, place a rice paper onto a shallow tray or plate and pour over hot water. Make sure the rice paper is totally submerged. When soft, lift it out, shake off any excess water and lay it on the kitchen towel, smoothing out the edges.

Divide the crab mix into 8 portions. In the bottom centre of a rice paper, pile up one portion of the crab mix along with a few slices of mango and avocado. Roll tightly from the bottom. Halfway up, fold the sides inwards. Continue rolling until you have a tight parcel. Just before you are ready to serve, slice each roll into two with a sharp knife.

tuna, daikon & wasabi rolls

7.5-cm/3-in. piece of cucumber,
  deseeded and cut into
  matchsticks

7.5-cm/3-in. piece of daikon
  radish, cut into matchsticks

3 spring onions/scallions,
  cut into matchsticks

4 teaspoons mayonnaise

1 teaspoon wasabi paste

freshly squeezed lime juice, to taste

80 g/3 oz. sashimi-grade
  tuna steak

2 tablespoons soy sauce

8 x 18-cm/7-in. rice papers

a few fresh coriander/
  cilantro leaves

sesame seeds (optional)

Makes 16

Lay the cucumber, radish and spring onions/scallions on paper towels.

Mix together the mayonnaise and wasabi, and add lime juice to taste

Cut the tuna into 8 strips and put it on a plate. Sprinkle over the soy sauce.

Lay out a clean kitchen towel. One by one, place a rice paper onto a shallow tray or plate and pour over hot water. Make sure the rice paper is totally submerged. When soft, lift it out, shake off any excess water and lay it on the kitchen towel, smoothing out the edges.

Divide the ingredients into 8 portions. In the bottom centre of a rice paper, place a couple of coriander/cilantro leaves, then pile up one portion of ingredients and spoon a little wasabi mayo on top. Sprinkle with sesame seeds and roll tightly from the bottom. Halfway up, fold the sides inwards. Continue rolling until you have a tight parcel. Just before you are ready to serve, slice each roll into two with a sharp knife.

yee sang rolls

These rolls are inspired by the interactive, must-have dish for Chinese New Year celebrations, 'Yee Sang'.

Traditionally, all of the ingredients are piled on a plate, then everyone uses their chopsticks to toss the shredded vegetables into the air and shouts out their dreams and aspirations. It's believed that the higher you toss, the greater your fortunes!

I simply fell in love with the flavours, so I put them in summer rolls.

You can add a little raw fish or smoked salmon if you wish but I love this vegetarian version. You can prepare all of the ingredients ahead and refrigerate, but only make the rolls up to half an hour before serving.

10-cm/4-in. piece of cucumber,
   skin on, deseeded
⅓ pomelo (or ½ pink grapefruit),
   cut into segments
3 spring onions/scallions,
   cut into matchsticks
10-cm/4-in. piece of daikon
   radish, cut into matchsticks
10-cm/4-in. piece of carrot,
   cut into matchsticks
4-cm/1½-in. piece of fresh
   ginger, cut into matchsticks

For the sauce
½ teaspoon sesame oil
3 tablespoons plum sauce
3 teaspoons toasted sesame seeds
a small handful of toasted
   peanuts, finely chopped
½ teaspoon Chinese five spice
a pinch of white pepper
a squeeze of fresh lime juice,
   to taste
8 x 18-cm/7-in. rice papers

Makes 16

Put the cucumber and pomelo on a few sheets of paper towels to soak up any excess liquid.

Mix together the ingredients for the sauce in a small bowl.

Lay out a clean kitchen towel. One by one, place a rice paper onto a shallow tray or plate and pour over hot water. Make sure the rice paper is totally submerged. When soft, lift it out, shake off any excess water and lay it on the kitchen towel, smoothing out the edges.

Divide the ingredients into 8 portions. In the bottom centre of a rice paper, pile up one portion. Spoon on a little sauce and roll tightly from the bottom. Halfway up, fold the sides inwards. Continue rolling until you have a tight parcel. Just before you are ready to serve, slice each roll into two with a sharp knife.

Top to bottom: tuna, daikon & wasabi rolls (p80), yee sang rolls (p81), crab, mango & avocado rolls (p80).

teriyaki salmon skewers

2 garlic cloves, thinly sliced

thumb-sized piece of fresh ginger,
    thinly sliced on the diagonal

freshly squeezed juice of ½ a lime

1 teaspoon sesame oil

5 tablespoons Japanese soy sauce

4 tablespoons clear honey

500 g/1 lb. 2 oz. salmon fillet,
    skinned and boned

black sesame seeds to garnish

26 wooden/metal skewers

a baking sheet, greased

Makes 26

Put the garlic, ginger, lime juice, sesame oil, soy and honey in a large bowl. Stir well to combine.

Slice the salmon into 26 bite-sized pieces. Toss the salmon in the sauce.

Preheat the oven to 190°C (375°F) Gas 5.

After 10 minutes, drain the salmon and reserve the sauce. Skewer the salmon and place on the prepared baking sheet and cook in the preheated oven for 5 minutes, or until cooked to your liking. Meanwhile, reduce the sauce in a small saucepan on a low-medium heat for about 3 minutes, or until thickened and glossy.

Remove the skewers from the oven and brush or spoon the reduced sauce over each salmon piece, along with a sprinkling of sesame seeds. Serve immediately.

gochujang chicken skewers

Gochujang is a wonderful chilli paste from Korea. It has a deep, earthy flavour from fermented soya beans and a rounded kick from chilli powder. It finds its way into a lot of dishes I cook at home, and always into chicken wings. If you can find its partner in crime 'doenjang' try replacing half the soy with a teaspoon of it.

500 g/1 lb. 2 oz. chicken
    thighs, skinless and
    boneless, cut into 40
    pieces

sesame seeds and thinly
    sliced spring
    onions/scallions,
    to garnish

For the marinade

2 garlic cloves, grated

thumb-sized piece of fresh
    ginger, grated

2 tablespoons soy sauce

1 teaspoon sesame oil

1 tablespoon white wine
    vinegar

1 tablespoon clear honey,
    plus extra to taste

1 heaped teaspoon
    medium-hot Korean
    Gochujang paste

20 wooden/metal skewers

a baking sheet, greased

Makes 20

Combine all of the ingredients for the marinade in a large bowl. Add the chicken pieces to the bowl and leave to marinate for no more than 20 minutes.

Preheat the oven to 190°C (375°F) Gas 5.

Put 2 pieces of chicken onto each skewer and lay them on the prepared baking sheet. Cook the chicken for 10–12 minutes.

While the chicken is cooking, reduce the marinade in a small saucepan on a low-medium heat for about 3 minutes, adding a little more honey to taste.

When the chicken is cooked, brush or spoon the sauce on top and sprinkle with the sesame seeds and spring onions/scallions.

mini okonomiyaki

I had my first Okonomiyaki at my friend Reiko's home, one cold evening. It was like a big, warm, umami hug in the form of a savoury pancake. Okonomiyaki does taste best with dashi and okonomiyaki sauce (I like the Bulldog brand). However, you can use chicken stock and brown sauce/steak sauce respectively as substitutes.

1 egg
125 ml/½ cup of dashi stock
* (1 teaspoon of dashi*
* powder in 125 ml/½ cup*
* of water)*
60 g/½ cup plain/
* all-purpose flour*
150 g/5 oz. cabbage,
* finely shredded*
5 spring onions/scallions,
* finely chopped*
2 thin slices of bacon,
* cooked and finely chopped*
3 tablespoons vegetable oil

For the garnish
okonomiyaki sauce, to taste
Japanese Kewpie
* mayonnaise (or regular*
* mayonnaise in a squeezy*
* bottle), to taste*
bonito flakes or shredded
* spring onion/scallions,*
* to sprinkle*

Makes 15

Beat the egg in a large bowl and lightly whisk in the stock. Slowly whisk in the flour, ensuring there are no lumps.

Add the cabbage, spring onions/scallions and bacon to the bowl.

Put a non-stick frying pan/skillet on a medium heat and add half the oil. When hot, add a heaped teaspoon of pancake mix to the pan and cook for a couple of minutes on each side before transferring to paper towels. Squeeze over a little sauce and mayonnaise and top with a pinch of bonito flakes or spring onions/scallions.

miso-glazed aubergine skewers

2 large aubergines/eggplants or
* 10 mini aubergines/eggplants*
* (mini aubergines, shown*
* opposite, look prettier but large*
* aubergines/eggplants taste better)*
3 tablespoons sunflower oil

For the glaze
2 tablespoons (dark) miso paste
3 tablespoons mirin
1 teaspoon caster/granulated sugar

To decorate
sesame seeds or finely sliced
* spring onions/scallions*

40 mini wooden skewers

Makes 40

Combine all of the ingredients for the glaze in a small saucepan and whisk over a medium heat for a couple of minutes until the sugar has dissolved.

Preheat the oven to 180°C (350°F) Gas 4.

Slice each large aubergine/eggplant lengthways into 4 pieces, then cut each quarter into 5 pieces. If using mini aubergines, cut each crossways into 4 pieces.

Brush both sides with a little sunflower oil, place on a baking sheet and bake for 10 minutes in the preheated oven, or until just cooked through.

Remove from the oven and preheat a grill/broiler.

Brush the glaze over each piece of aubergine/eggplant and grill/broil for a minute or so until the glaze starts to bubble. Be careful, it can burn easily.

Remove from the grill/broiler, skewer a piece of aubergine onto each skewer, sprinkle with sesame seeds or spring onions/scallions and serve.

thai fish cakes

These flavourful and juicy fish cakes take minutes to whizz up in a food processor. You can make them ahead of time, cover them in clingfilm/plastic wrap and refrigerate overnight or freeze a week ahead.

5 spring onions/scallions,
   roughly chopped
600 g/1 lb. 5 oz. skinned and
   boned white fish (such as cod,
   coley or hake)
a handful of fresh coriander/cilantro
3 teaspoons fish sauce
3 tablespoons Thai red curry paste
1 teaspoon chopped lime leaves
100 g/3½ oz. French beans,
   finely chopped
4 tablespoons groundnut/peanut oil
sweet chilli/chili sauce, to serve

Makes 30

Blitz the spring onions/scallions in a food processor.

Cut the fish into chunks and add to the spring onions/scallions.

Blitz together with the coriander/cilantro, fish sauce, curry paste and lime leaves until you have a paste.

Empty the contents into a bowl, mix in the beans and mould into bite-sized balls, slightly flattening them.

Heat the oil in a frying pan/skillet and when very hot, fry the fish cakes in batches for a minute or so on each side until cooked through.

Remove, drain quickly on paper towels and serve while still hot with a bowl of sweet chilli/chili sauce.

coconut calamari

Crunchy, tender squid with a little heat. This one is a real party pleaser.

8 baby squid
1 x 400-ml/14-oz. can coconut milk
50 g/2 oz. desiccated coconut
100 g/3½ oz. cornflour/cornstarch
1 teaspoon salt
1½ teaspoons cayenne pepper
500 ml/2 cups sunflower or
   peanut/ groundnut oil
sweet chilli/chili sauce, to serve
1 tablespoon freshly chopped
   coriander/cilantro (optional)
chopped red chillies/chiles,
   to garnish

Makes 40

Pull out the tentacles and cut each squid into 4 rings.

Place the rings and tentacles into a bowl and cover with the coconut milk. Refrigerate for at least 2 hours.

In a large bowl, mix together the cornflour/cornstarch, desiccated coconut, salt and cayenne pepper.

Heat the oil in a medium saucepan until it reaches 170°C–180°C (325°F–350°F), or until a flick of flour sizzles when dropped in the pan.

Drain the squid and lightly toss it in the flour mix.

Fry in batches for a few minutes or until the batter is crunchy. Drain on paper towels.

Serve with sweet chilli/chili sauce, mixed with the coriander/cilantro, if using.

crab, chilli & lime filo tartlets

3 sheets of filo/phyllo pastry
  (about 135 g/4¾ oz.)
100 g/1 stick minus 1 tablespoon
  unsalted butter, melted

Crab filling

400 g/1¾ cups fresh, cooked white
  crabmeat
5 spring onions/scallions
10 g/½ cup fresh coriander/cilantro
2 red chillies/chiles, deseeded
4 tablespoons mayonnaise
freshly squeezed juice of 2 limes
Tabasco sauce, to season (optional)

12-hole muffin pan, buttered

Makes 40

Preheat the oven to 180°C (350°F) Gas 4.

Stack the filo/phyllo sheets in a pile and use a sharp knife to cut them into 40 6-cm/2½-in. squares, each of which will have 3 layers of pastry. Keeping all other filo/phyllo squares covered with clingfilm/plastic wrap to prevent them drying out, take one set of 3 three squares. Lay one square onto a chopping board and brush lightly with melted butter. Top with a second square, offset to allow corners to show. Brush lightly with melted butter and repeat with the final square.

Gently press the layered pastry into the hole of the muffin pan and repeat to fill the pan. Bake in the preheated oven for 8–10 minutes, until golden brown. Cool and store in an airtight container until required. Repeat with the remaining pastry.

To make the crab filling, drain the crabmeat and place in a bowl. Chop the spring onions/scallions, coriander/cilantro and chillies/chiles very finely. Mix with the mayonnaise and season with lime juice, Tabasco, salt and white pepper.

Fill each tart with the crab filling and serve immediately.

....

asian slaw & prawn tartlets

¼ red cabbage
¼ white cabbage
1 Gala apple, peeled
1 large carrot, peeled
1 spring onion/scallion
1 fresh red chilli/chile,
  deseeded
1 teaspoon salt
1 tablespoon sour cream
  or mayonnaise
17 cooked and shelled
  prawns/shrimp
34 filo/phyllo baskets
  (see above)

For the dressing

2 limes
1 teaspoon caster/
  granulated sugar
3 teaspoons fish sauce
2 teaspoons soy sauce

Makes 34

Mix all of the ingredients for the dressing in a bowl. Set aside.

Either using a mandoline or sharp knife, slice the red cabbage very finely and place in a bowl. Shred the white cabbage, apple, carrot, spring onion/scallion and chilli/chile in the same way and place in a separate bowl.

Season both bowls with ½ teaspoon salt and mix well. Add half the dressing to one bowl and the other half to the second bowl, let sit for at least 10 minutes but no longer than 30 minutes.

Drain the vegetables and mix together just before serving so that the red cabbage doesn't turn everything pink. Add the sour cream.

Spoon a little slaw into each filo/phyllo basket and top with half a prawn/shrimp. You can pinch the ends of the prawns/shrimp together to add height.

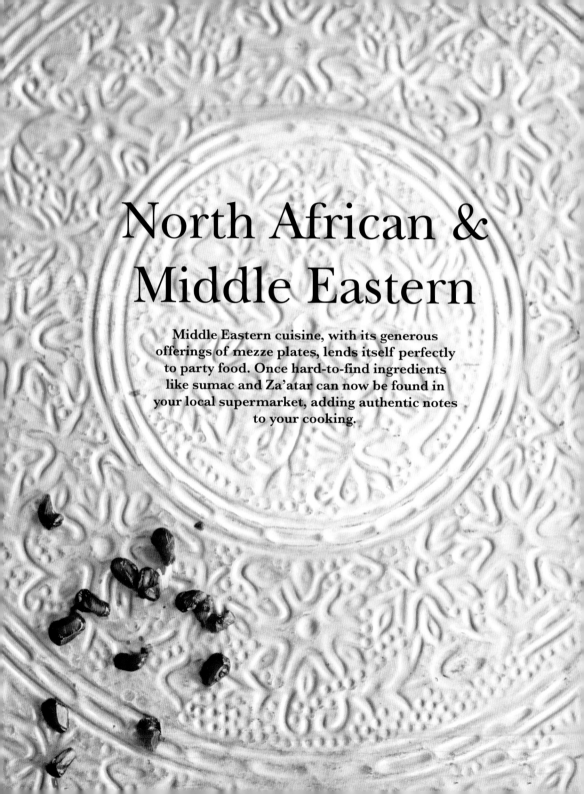

North African & Middle Eastern

Middle Eastern cuisine, with its generous
offerings of mezze plates, lends itself perfectly
to party food. Once hard-to-find ingredients
like sumac and Za'atar can now be found in
your local supermarket, adding authentic notes
to your cooking.

kofte

500 g/1 lb. 2 oz. minced/ground
  lamb, shoulder is best
1½ teaspoons ground cumin
¼ teaspoon ground allspice
1 egg
50 g/2 oz. pine nuts, toasted
2 tablespoons freshly chopped
  flat-leaf parsley
1 tablespoon freshly chopped mint
½ teaspoon ground cinnamon
1 teaspoon salt
1 onion, very finely chopped
about 800 ml/scant 3½ cups
  vegetable oil

30 wooden skewers (optional)

Makes 30

Combine all of the ingredients in a bowl and mix thoroughly. Use two tablespoons to shape the lamb mixture into 30 even kofte, and set aside on a sheet of baking parchment as you shape each one.

Add enough vegetable oil to a deep, heavy saucepan to come to a depth of 5 cm/2 in. Heat the oil to 180°C (350°F). Fry one kofte for 3–4 minutes, turning half-way through cooking, until cooked through and browned. Allow the kofte to cool slightly then taste to check the seasoning. Season the rest of the kofte with extra salt, if necessary.

Cook the remaining kofte, in batches, and drain on paper towels. Insert a wooden skewer into each kofte, if you like.

persian sausage rolls

375 g/13 oz. ready-rolled puff
  pastry
1 egg, beaten

sausage mix
1 tablespoon olive oil
½ red onion, finely diced
400 g/14 oz. sausagemeat
45 g/1½ oz. chopped pistachios
25 g/1 oz. barberries
½ teaspoon sumac
½ teaspoon freshly ground
  black pepper
½ teaspoon ground cinnamon
½ teaspoon ground cumin

a baking sheet, lined with
baking parchment

Makes 20–25

Heat the oil in a frying pan/skillet. Add the onion and sauté until caramelized. Cool and mix well with all of the other sausage-mix ingredients.

Lay the pastry sheet on a lightly floured surface and give it a little roll, if necessary, to make it 3 mm/⅛ in. thick. Cut it crossways into 3 strips.

Divide the sausage meat into 3 parts and press a line of sausagemeat down the middle of each strip of pastry, leaving 2.5 cm/1 in. free at each end.

Brush the length of the pastry with a little of the beaten egg on one side and roll the other side over the sausage to secure it in place. Pinch the ends of each roll together.

Transfer the rolls to the prepared baking sheet, brush them with more egg wash and pop them in the freezer for 15 minutes. Meanwhile, preheat the oven to 190°C (375°F) Gas 5.

Take the sausage rolls out of the freezer and cut each roll into 8 pieces.

If you have leftover egg wash, brush it on, spread the rolls out on the prepared baking sheet and bake for at least 20 minutes, or until golden.

za'atar roast chicken & sumac labneh lettuce cups

2 tablespoons olive oil

2 tablespoons za'atar

1 large garlic clove

salt and freshly ground
black pepper

4 boneless, skinless
chicken thighs

6 baby gem lettuces

170 ml/¾ cup labneh or
thick Greek/US strained
plain yogurt

freshly squeezed juice of
½ a lemon

¼ red onion, finely sliced

sumac, pomegranate seeds
and freshly chopped
coriander/cilantro,
to garnish

a baking sheet, lined with
baking parchment

Makes 32

Preheat the oven to 180°C (350°F) Gas 4.

Rub the olive oil, za'atar, garlic and seasoning onto the chicken thighs and place them on the prepared baking sheet. Roast in the oven for 20 minutes, making sure the thickest part of the thigh is cooked. Leave the chicken to cool in its juices for 10 minutes.

Cut the root end off the baby gem lettuces and pull apart the leaves.

Mix the labneh with the lemon juice and season to taste. Pull apart or slice each thigh into 8 pieces. Spoon a little labneh into each gem cup, followed by the chicken and some red onion. Sprinkle over a pinch of sumac, pomegranate seeds and chopped coriander/cilantro and serve.

moroccan chicken puffs

For the chicken mix

2 tablespoons olive oil

1 large onion, finely chopped

3 garlic cloves, crushed

½ teaspoon ground ginger

¼ teaspoon ground cinnamon

a small pinch of saffron

¼ teaspoon ground cumin

1 small preserved lemon,
quartered, seeds and
pith removed

4 chicken thighs, boned and
skinned and diced very small

¼ teaspoon smoked paprika

freshly ground black pepper

1 tablespoon freshly chopped
flat-leaf parsley

1 tablespoon freshly chopped
coriander/cilantro

500 g/1 lb. 2 oz. puff pastry

1 egg, beaten

sesame seeds, for sprinkling

7.5-cm/3-in. pastry/
cookie cutter

a baking sheet, lined with
baking parchment

Makes 30–35

Preheat the oven to 180°C (350°F) Gas 4.

For the chicken mix, heat the oil in a frying pan/skillet and sauté the onion and garlic for 5 minutes. Add all of the other chicken mix ingredients to the pan. When the chicken is cooked, cool for a few minutes before seasoning with black pepper and adding the fresh herbs.

Once completely cooled, roll out the puff pastry until 3 mm/⅛ in. thick and use the pastry/cookie cutter to cut it into rounds.

Place 1 teaspoonful of the chicken mix in the middle of each disk and then pinch the edges together, like a dumpling. Place the puffs pinch-side down on the prepared baking sheet 2.5 cm/1 in. apart and brush the tops with the beaten egg. Sprinkle with sesame seeds and bake in the oven for 15–20 minutes until golden.

This page: za'atar roast chicken & sumac labneh lettuce cups (p95), kofte (p94).
Opposite: persian sausage rolls (p94), moroccan chicken puffs (p95).

borek
with mint & honey

200 g/7 oz. feta cheese, crumbled

1 tablespoon natural/plain yogurt

1 teaspoon freshly chopped flat-leaf
parsley

grated zest of ½ lemon

freshly ground black pepper

3 filo/phyllo sheets

50 g/3 tablespoons unsalted butter

olive oil, for frying

1 tablespoon runny honey, to serve

1 teaspoon shredded fresh mint,
to serve

Makes 18

Combine the feta, yogurt, parsley and lemon zest in a bowl. Season to taste with the black pepper.

Cut each filo/phyllo sheet into 6 and place a teaspoon of the feta mix onto the base of each strip, leaving a 2.5-cm/1-in. gap around the edge. Cover any filo/phyllo you are not using with a damp kitchen towel.

Melt the butter and brush a little around the edges, roll up and tuck the sides into a cigar, securing the end flap with more melted butter. You can keep these in the refrigerator until they are ready to cook.

Add 1 tablespoon of oil to a frying pan/skillet and fry the borek for 3 minutes over medium heat, turning occasionally, until crisp. You will need to do this in batches, adding a little more oil to the pan each time.

Leave to stand for a few minutes as the melted cheese will be very hot. Serve with a drizzle of honey and shredded mint.

baba ganoush

4 large aubergines/eggplants

3 garlic cloves, crushed

freshly squeezed juice of 1 lemon

5 tablespoons tahini

4 tablespoons olive oil

salt and freshly ground
black pepper

Makes 800–900 g/1¾–2 lb.

Pierce the aubergines/eggplant a few times with a skewer.

Place an aubergine/eggplant on each gas ring of your hob/stovetop and grill over the open flame, rotating every few minutes with tongs. Alternatively, place the aubergine/eggplant under a preheated overhead grill/broiler and grill/broil until the skin is completely charred and the flesh soft. This will take around 15 minutes.

Transfer the aubergines/eggplant to a plate covered in foil. Leave for 10 minutes, or until cool enough to handle.

Carefully scrape the flesh out of each aubergine/eggplant and pulse it in a food processor, along with the crushed garlic, lemon juice, tahini and olive oil. Season to taste with salt and pepper. The baba ganoush will keep for up to 3 days in an airtight container in the fridge.

dates stuffed
with goat's cheese, pistachios & pomegranate

20 pitted dates
80 g/3 oz. soft goat's cheese
2 tablespoons slivered pistachios
grated zest of 1 orange
2 tablespoons pomegranate seeds

Makes 20

Split the dates in half and fill them with the goat's cheese.

Sprinkle over the pistachios, orange zest and pomegranate seeds, and serve.

harissa aubergine fritters

1 aubergine/eggplant
about 800 ml/28 fl. oz.
*   sunflower oil, for frying*
120 g/1 cup minus
*   1½ tablespoons gram*
*   flour/chickpea flour*
3 teaspoons rose harissa
*   (or regular harissa if you*
*   can't find rose harissa)*
2 tablespoons fresh
*   coriander/ cilantro,*
*   roughly chopped*

a large pinch of salt
1 teaspoon freshly ground
*   white pepper*
2 teaspoons smoked paprika
coriander chutney or minty
*   yogurt dip, to serve (see*
*   page 64)*

Makes 30–35

Heat the oil in a deep, heavy-bottomed saucepan to 180°C (350°F).

Slice the aubergine in half lengthways, then slice into 5-mm/¼-in. semi circles.

Mix the gram flour/chickpea flour, harissa, coriander/cilantro, salt pepper and paprika in a bowl. Add 140 ml/scant ⅔ cup water and whisk until you have a batter the consistency of single/light cream – you may need to add more water.

Dip the aubergines/eggplants in the batter with a fork and drop them into the hot oil, in batches. Turn after 2 minutes and cook for 2 minutes more, until the batter is golden and crisp. Drain on paper towels and serve with chutney or minty yogurt dip.

baba ganoush & feta endives

4 red endives
1 quantity baba ganoush
*   (see opposite)*
160 g/5½ oz. feta cheese,
*   crumbled*

10 freshly chopped mint
*   leaves*
seeds of ½ a pomegranate

Makes about 32

Chop the bottom off each endive and carefully peel it apart.

Put a heaped teaspoonful of the baba ganoush onto the end of each endive.

Sprinkle over the feta cheese, mint leaves and pomegranate seeds and serve.

From left to right: dates stuffed with goat's cheese, pistachios & pomegranate (p99), baba ganoush & feta endives (p99), harissa aubergine fritters (p99), borek with mint & honey (p98).

The Americas

There's so much variety in this chapter, from light and zesty ceviche to filling and comforting quesadillas and pulled pork. I love the homemade Jamaican food of my brother-in-law, Chris, and his dad, Felix. While I haven't figured out how to make Felix's amazing ackee and saltfish into a canape, I had to include a little jerk in the book, as no summer party feels right without it.

sea bass ceviche, lychee & chilli

⅛ red onion, finely chopped

freshly squeezed juice of 1 lime

200 g/7 oz. fresh seabass, cut into
  1 x 2-cm/½ x ¾-in. pieces

10g/1 tablespoon fresh red
  chilli/chile, finely chopped

3 lychees, diced

½ mango, diced

3 shakes of Tabasco

½ teaspoon salt

olive oil

25 canapé spoons

Makes 25

Put the finely chopped red onion and lime juice in a large mixing bowl and set aside for 20 minutes.

Add the remaining ingredients to the bowl, cover and leave to marinate for 20 minutes.

Serve on canapé spoons or tortilla chips.

tequila scallops

1 tablespoon olive oil

2 shallots, finely diced

1 teaspoon unsalted butter

200 g/7 oz. scallops, finely diced

freshly squeezed juice of 1 lime

1 tablespoon tequila

salt, to taste

freshly chopped amaranth or baby
  coriander/cilantro, to garnish

15 canapé spoons

Makes 15

Heat the olive oil in a frying pan/skillet. Add the shallots and sauté over high heat until the edges are crisp.

Remove the shallots from the pan and put the pan back on high heat.

Add the butter to the pan, followed by the scallops. Let the scallops brown on one side, then turn over.

Add half of the lime juice and the tequila. Put the shallots back in the pan and cook with the scallops for a few minutes, until the scallops are just cooked. Taste for seasoning; you may want to add more salt or lime.

Serve immediately on canapé spoons with your chosen herb garnish. The scallops are best hot but can also be served at room temperature.

tuna & wasabi ceviche

½ teaspoon soy sauce

130 g/4½ oz. sashimi-grade
  tuna steak, cut into
  1-cm/½-in. cubes

1 tablespoon freshly
  squeezed lime juice

1 avocado, cut into
  1-cm/½-in. cubes

1 tablespoon mayonnaise

1 teaspoon wasabi

10-cm/4-in. piece
  of cucumber

1 spring onion/scallion,
  finely sliced, to garnish

garlic cress, to garnish

20 canapé spoons

Makes 20

In a bowl, sprinkle the soy sauce over the tuna and toss to mix. In a separate bowl, sprinkle the lime juice over the avocado cubes.

Peel the cucumber and scrape out the seeds, so you are left with firm flesh. Cut the cucumber into 1-cm/½-in. cubes and mix into the avocado, along with the wasabi and mayonnaise. Gently stir in the tuna.

Spoon onto the canapé spoons and garnish with sliced spring onion/scallion and garlic cress.

jerk chicken & plantain skewers

500 g/17½ oz. boneless,
  skinless chicken thighs
2 ripe plantains
2 tablespoons sunflower oil

For the marinade
1 tablespoon freshly
  chopped thyme leaves
1 Scotch bonnet, deseeded
  (or 2 red chillies/
  chiles, seeds in)
5 spring onions/scallions,
  roughly chopped
1 teaspoon salt
1 tablespoon soy sauce
3 large garlic cloves
thumb-sized piece of fresh

ginger, grated
2 tablespoons white
  wine vinegar
1 tablespoon soft light
  brown sugar
1 teaspoon ground allspice
1 teaspoon freshly ground
  black pepper
1 teaspoon ground
  cinnamon
½ teaspoon freshly grated
  nutmeg
36 mini wooden skewers

Makes 36

Whizz all the marinade ingredients in a food processor until smooth.

Cut each chicken thigh into 6, place in a bowl and cover with the marinade. Cover and refrigerate for at least 6 hours or overnight.

Cut the plantains down the middle, lengthways, and then into 1-cm/½-in. pieces.

When ready to serve, cook the chicken pieces on a very hot griddle pan for a few minutes on each side until cooked in the middle. Transfer to a warm plate.

Heat the oil in a frying pan/skillet. Sauté the plantain in two batches for 2 minutes on each side.

Skewer the chicken and plantain and serve.

jamaican-spiced prawn & mango skewers

170 g/6 oz. raw, shelled
  prawns/shrimp
1 tablespoon sunflower oil
1 mango
a handful of fresh
  coriander/cilantro
freshly squeezed juice of
  1 lime

For the curry powder
1 teaspoon fennel seeds
1 teaspoon fenugreek seeds
1 teaspoon mustard seeds

2 tablespoons coriander
  seeds
1 tablespoon cumin seeds
1 teaspoon ground allspice
2 tablespoons ground
  turmeric

a spice grinder or pestle
and mortar
25 mini wooden skewers

Makes 25

To make the curry powder, put all the spices except the allspice and turmeric in a frying pan/skillet, and cook over medium heat for a few minutes, until fragrant but not darkened.

Let cool and transfer to a spice grinder or pestle and mortar, and grind. Add the allspice and turmeric.

Sprinkle the prawns/shrimp with 1 heaped teaspoon of the curry powder and a little oil. Mix and leave to marinate in the refrigerator for at least 2 hours.

Slice the mango into 2.5-cm/1-in. squares, 6 mm/¼ in. deep.

Heat the sunflower oil in a frying pan/skillet, add the prawns/shrimp and sauté for a few minutes, until cooked through.

Place a coriander/cilantro leaf on top of each mango cube and sprinkle over a little lime juice. Top each with a prawn/shrimp and skewer.

NOTE this makes 4 times the curry powder you will need, so if you are making more than 25 skewers you will not need to multiply the curry powder.

pulled pork on cornbread muffins

1 onion, thinly sliced

2 tablespoons salt

2 tablespoons muscovado sugar

2 teaspoons smoked paprika

2 teaspoons ground cumin

1.5 kg/3¼ lb. pork shoulder,
    bone in and skin on

liquid smoke

coriander/cilantro and red onion
    slices, to garnish

Cornbread muffins

150 g/1 cup fine cornmeal

130 g/1 cup plain/all-purpose flour

4 tablespoons caster/granulated
    sugar

1 teaspoon salt

1 tablespoon baking powder

2 eggs

235 ml/1 cup buttermilk

6 tablespoons vegetable oil

2 x 24-hole mini muffin pans,
greased

Makes 40

Preheat the oven to 200°C (400°F) Gas 6.

Line a small roasting pan with enough foil overhanging to wrap around the meat. Place the sliced onions in the pan.

Rub the salt, sugar, paprika and cumin into the meat and sit it on top of the onions. Place in the oven, with the foil open, for 30 minutes.

Spray the meat with liquid smoke (no more than a teaspoon), and wrap the foil over the meat. Reduce the oven to 120°C (250°F) Gas½ and cook for 4–5 hours, until the meat is falling apart.

Remove the meat from the oven and let sit for 30 minutes, then pull the meat off the bone with 2 forks. Leave it in the juices and onions and refrigerate until needed.

For the cornbread muffins, preheat the oven to 190°C (375°F) Gas 5.

Mix the cornmeal, flour, sugar, salt and baking powder in one bowl. In a separate bowl, whisk the eggs with the buttermilk and vegetable oil. Pour the wet mixture into the dry ingredients and mix until just combined. Do not over-mix.

Using a teaspoon, drop a spoonful of the mixture into each hole of the muffin pan. Bake in the preheated oven for 8 minutes, or until cooked through. Let cool on a wire rack.

To serve, reheat the pork in the oven and slice the top off each muffin. Place a spoonful of pork on each muffin and garnish with coriander/cilantro or red onion slices.

black bean quesadillas

1 tablespoon olive oil

1 large red onion, finely
    diced

6 flour tortillas,
    approximately 20 cm/
    8 in. in diameter

220 g/8 oz. grated Cheddar
    cheese

1 fresh red chilli/chile,
    finely diced

a small handful of freshly
    chopped coriander/
    cilantro, plus a few extra
    leaves to garnish

150 g/1 cup cooked black
    beans, drained and
    rinsed

Makes 36

Heat the olive oil in a frying pan/skillet. Add the onion and sauté for a few minutes until softened.

Spread out three tortillas and sprinkle with cheese, onion, beans, coriander/cilantro and chilli/chile.

Place the other three tortillas on top. Fry them, one by one, in a hot non-stick griddle pan or frying pan/skillet for a few minutes on each side, until the tortilla is crisp and the cheese has melted.

Cut each quesadilla into 12 wedges and serve with a sprinkle of coriander/cilantro leaves.

chilli con carne cups

You can make the chilli con carne up to 3 days before you plan to serve these canapés.

2 tablespoons olive oil

200 g/7 oz. good-quality
  minced/ground beef
  (not lean) or chuck steak,
  cut into small pieces

1 small onion, diced

2 garlic cloves, crushed

300 ml/1¼ cups beef stock
  or water

200 g/7 oz. canned chopped
  tomatoes

2 tablespoons tomato
  purée/paste

¼ teaspoon chipotle paste

½ teaspoon chilli flakes/hot
  pepper flakes (habanero if
  you can)

½ teaspoon unsweetened cocoa
  powder

40 g/¼ cup cooked red kidney
  beans or black beans,
  drained and rinsed

30 store-bought 'croustades'
  or mini pastry cups

100 g/3½ oz. shredded red
  cabbage or diced avocado

freshly squeezed lime juice,
  for squeezing

fresh coriander/cilantro,
  to garnish (optional)

Makes 30

Heat a tablespoon of oil in a large frying pan/skillet and brown the meat over medium/high heat. Transfer the meat to a bowl and, in the same pan, fry the onions and the garlic in a little more oil for about 5 minutes, until softened.

Return the meat to the pan and add the stock, canned tomatoes, tomato purée/paste, chipotle paste and chilli flakes/hot pepper flakes, and cook for 40 minutes or so, until most of the liquid has been absorbed and the meat is tender.

Add the beans and cocoa, and heat through. Season to taste with salt and pepper. For best results, allow to cool then refrigerate, covered, for up to 3 days.

When ready to serve, add a teaspoonful of the chilli con carne to each croustade or pastry cup and garnish with a pinch of red cabbage or cube of avocado, a squeeze of lime and a little fresh coriander/cilantro, if you like.

From left to right: chilli con carne cups
(p109), black bean quesadillas (p108),
pulled pork on cornbread muffins (p108).

empanadillas (mini empanadas)

The best food I've ever eaten at a party were the empanadas at the home of my Paraguayan friend Carmen. That's all she served. There were two options: spinach and ricotta or chilli con carne. Along with a pile of paper napkins, some cold beers and a few bottles of Tabasco, everyone was set for a perfect evening. Sometimes less is more. This amount of pastry allows for 30 spinach and ricotta and 30 chilli con carne empanadas. Halve the recipe if you are only cooking one or the other. The pastry freezes very well.

250 g/2 sticks plus
  2 tablespoons unsalted
  butter, chilled
450 g/3¼ cups plain/
  all-purpose flour
1 egg
60 ml/¼ cup cold water
½ teaspoon salt
1 quantity filling (see below)
1 egg, beaten

7.5-cm/3-in. pastry/cookie
cutter

Makes 60

Cut the butter into small cubes. Place all of the ingredients except the beaten egg into the food processor and blitz until a dough forms. Add a little more water if the dough doesn't come together. Wrap the dough in clingfilm/plastic wrap and refrigerate for 30 minutes.

Preheat the oven to 200°C (400°F) Gas 6.

Roll out the dough to 3 mm/⅛ in. thick. Use the cutter to stamp out disks. Lay the disks out on a lightly floured surface and put a heaped teaspoon of filling in the middle.

Moisten the top half of the dough with a little water. Pull over the other half of dough, taking care to squeeze out any air. You can do this by pressing down on the edge of the dough with the tines of a fork or by folding and pinching the edges over.

Place on a baking sheet, brush with a little of the beaten egg and bake in the preheated oven for 15–20 minutes, or until golden.

spinach & ricotta filling

20 g/1 generous tablespoon
  unsalted butter
150 g/5 oz. fresh spinach
1 tablespoon olive oil
½ onion, finely chopped
1 garlic clove, crushed
20 g/1 oz. freshly grated
  Parmesan

160 g/5½ oz. ricotta
  (drained)
½ beaten egg
a pinch of salt
½ teaspoon freshly grated
  nutmeg

Makes 30

Add the butter to a small saucepan, along with the spinach and a splash of water. Cover and leave to steam for a few minutes. When wilted, drain in a sieve/strainer and chop finely. Place in a large bowl.

In the same pan, add the olive oil and sauté the onion and garlic. Add the onion and garlic to the spinach. When cool, add the cheeses and egg. Season with salt and nutmeg. Use in the recipe above.

chilli con carne filling

1 quantity Chilli con Carne **Makes 30**
  (see page 109)

Use the filling in the recipe above.

Sweet Bites

If you are anything like me, a party doesn't
feel celebratory without some sort of cake.
From mini desserts in shot glasses, cocktails
in jelly form to elegant bites, end your party
on a sweet note!

chocolate & espresso pots

The espresso intensifies the chocolate, but is, in itself, a surprisingly subtle flavour. These pots are very rich and luxurious.

200 g/7 oz. dark/
  bittersweet (70%)
  chocolate, chopped
400 ml/1¾ cups double/
  heavy cream
3 tablespoons espresso
2 teaspoons vanilla
  bean paste
3 tablespoons muscovado/
  turbinado sugar
a small pinch of salt

20 g/1 oz. cocoa nibs/
  chocolate shavings,
  to serve
150 ml/generous ½ cup
  double/heavy cream,
  whipped (optional)

15 shot glasses or espresso cups

Makes 15

Put the chocolate in a large heatproof bowl. Heat the cream, espresso, vanilla paste, sugar and salt in a saucepan, stirring to combine.

When it begins to simmer, take off the heat and pour over the chocolate. Let it sit for 1 minute, then whisk until smooth and glossy.

Pour into shot glasses, cover with clingfilm/plastic wrap and leave to set overnight, or for at least 2 hours.

Decorate with cocoa nibs or chocolate shavings before serving, and add a teaspoonful of whipped cream to each one, if you like.

sweet chestnut & chocolate baskets

60 g/4 tablespoons softened,
  unsalted butter
85 g/¾ cup icing/confectioners'
  sugar
½ teaspoon vanilla bean paste
1 egg white, beaten
50 g/generous ⅓ cup
  plain/all-purpose flour
2 teaspoons unsweetened
  cocoa powder

For the chestnut cream
150 g/5 oz. sweet chestnut purée
5 tablespoons cream cheese
270 ml/1¼ cups double/heavy cream

a piping/pastry bag
a 24-hole mini muffin pan, greased
a silicone sheet

Makes 30

Begin by making the basket tuiles. Use an electric hand-held whisk to combine the butter, sugar and vanilla in a bowl. Add the egg white. Slowly add the flour and cocoa and whisk. Refrigerate for at least 30 minutes.

Meanwhile, preheat the oven to 190°C (375°F) Gas 5.

To make the chestnut cream, place the sweet chestnut purée, cream cheese and cream into a bowl and whisk together until quite stiff. Spoon into a piping/pastry bag and refrigerate until needed.

Place a silicone sheet onto a heavy baking sheet. Use an offset palette knife/metal spatula to spread the basket tuile mixture into 7-cm/3-in. circles. The mix needs to be very thinly spread.

It is best to experiment with just one tuile at first. Place it in the preheated oven and bake for 4–5 minutes.

Slide a palette knife/metal spatula under the tuile and place it over one of the holes of the muffin pan. Gently push it into the hole of the muffin pan. It will cool, and take form in seconds.

Bake the baskets in batches. When cool and ready to serve, snip a tiny hole in the end of the piping bag and pipe the cream with quite some pressure into the basket cases in a squiggle shape. Serve immediately.

mini portuguese custard tarts

350 g/12 oz. puff pastry

For the custard
1 tablespoon cornflour/cornstarch
1 heaped teaspoon plain/
   all-purpose flour
150 ml/⅔ cup full-fat/whole milk
3 egg yolks
90 g/scant ½ cup
   caster/granulated sugar
1 teaspoon vanilla paste
a pinch of ground cinnamon

6-cm/2½-in. pastry/cookie cutter
a 24-hole mini muffin pan,
lightly greased

Makes 24

To make the custard, whisk the flours, milk and egg yolks together.

In a saucepan bring the sugar, 60 ml/¼ cup water, vanilla and cinnamon to the boil and whisk gently.

Take off the heat and slowly pour over the flour mix while whisking gently. Return to the heat, stirring with a spatula to thicken it ever so slightly to the consistency of single/light cream. Remove from the heat, leave to cool, then refrigerate.

Preheat the oven to 200°C (400°F) Gas 6.

Roll out the puff pastry on a flour-dusted surface until 3 mm/⅛ in. thick. Use the cutter to stamp out disks and gently push them into the muffin pan.

Spoon in the custard, leaving a tiny bit of space free at the top of the pastry (the custard will rise).

Cook in the preheated oven for 15–20 minutes, until the tops darken. Remove and let cool on a wire rack.

chocolate & almond raspberry cakes

125 g/4½ oz. dark/bittersweet
   (70%) chocolate, chopped
125 g/1 stick plus 1 tablespoon
   unsalted butter
3 eggs, separated
60 g/⅓ cup caster/granulated
   sugar
25 g/¼ cup ground almonds
a pinch of salt
1 teaspoon vanilla bean paste
150 g/5 oz. raspberries or
   kirsch-soaked cherries
icing/confectioners' sugar,
   for dusting

a 24-hole mini muffin pan,
greased

Makes 30

Preheat the oven to 170°C (325°F) Gas 3.

Melt the chocolate and butter together in a bowl placed over a saucepan of gently simmering water, making sure the base of the bowl does not touch the water.

Beat the egg yolks with the sugar until pale and fluffy, then pour into the cooled melted-chocolate mix. Add the ground almonds, salt and vanilla bean paste and stir through.

In a large, clean bowl, whisk the egg whites until they form stiff peaks. Stir a third of the egg whites into the chocolate and mix until well combined. Use a large metal spoon to lightly fold in the rest of the egg whites until just combined.

Spoon the mix into the prepared muffin pan, gently place a raspberry or kirsch-soaked cherry on each cake and bake for 15 minutes, until a skewer inserted into the middle of a cake comes out clean.

Leave for a few minutes before transferring to a wire rack to cool. Dust with icing/confectioners' sugar to serve.

This page: chocolate & almond raspberry cakes (p117), mini portuguese custard tarts (p117), sweet chestnut & chocolate baskets (p116).
Opposite: Chocolate & espresso pots (p116).

salted caramel brownies

For me, brownies must be ever so slightly undercooked and fudgy. I take inspiration from Emma's blog 'Poires au Chocolat' and sprinkle the swirls of caramel with cocoa nibs for a bitter crunch.

150 g/1 stick plus 2 tablespoons
    unsalted butter
200 g/7 oz. dark/bittersweet
    (70%) chocolate, chopped
4 eggs, beaten
200 g/1 cup plus 2 tablespoons
    light brown sugar
100 g/½ cup caster/granulated
    sugar
a pinch of salt
1 teaspoon vanilla paste/extract
80 g/⅔ cup plain/all-purpose
    flour, sifted
1 tablespoon cocoa nibs (optional)

For the salted caramel
100 g/½ cup caster/superfine
    sugar
3 tablespoons golden/light corn
    syrup
4 tablespoons double/heavy cream
30 g/2 tablespoons unsalted butter
a pinch of fleur de sel or flaky
    sea salt

23 x 23-cm/9 x 9-in. brownie pan, lined with baking parchment

Makes 40–50

Preheat the oven to 170°C (325°F) Gas 3.

For the salted caramel, put the sugar and syrup in a small saucepan over a medium heat. Swirl the pan but do not stir. When the sugar is a copper colour, take off the heat and slowly whisk in the cream. Add the butter and salt, and gently whisk. Set aside.

Melt the butter and chocolate in a heatproof bowl set over a saucepan of gently simmering water, taking care that the water is not in contact with the bowl. Transfer to a large bowl. Add the eggs, along with the sugars, salt and vanilla. Fold in the flour.

Pour into the prepared pan and smooth the top. Drizzle the caramel onto the surface and use a skewer to swirl it around. Sprinkle over the nibs, if using, and bake for about 20–25 minutes. It should still have a slight wobble in the centre. Cut into squares.

frangelico truffles

By cutting the truffles into squares, you can avoid contact with warm hands and produce little cubes that look a little different and homemade. I love the rich, nutty taste of Frangelico but by all means substitute with your favourite liqueur.

200 g/7 oz. dark/bittersweet (70%)
    chocolate, chopped
200 ml/generous ¾ cup
    double/heavy cream
5 tablespoons Frangelico
a pinch of salt
1 teaspoon vanilla bean paste
15 g/1 tablespoon unsalted butter

15 x 12.5-cm/6 x 5-in. plastic container

Makes 25

Put the chocolate in a heatproof bowl. Bring the cream to a gentle simmer and then pour over the chocolate. Leave for 30 seconds.

Whisk the cream and chocolate together, then add the rest of the ingredients and stir together.

Line the plastic container with clingfilm/plastic wrap and pour in the chocolate mix. Refrigerate overnight.

Turn out the truffle onto a board and use a sharp knife to cut it into squares. Dust with cocoa powder.

These truffles can be kept in the refrigerator for up to 1 week. Dust with extra cocoa powder before serving. They also freeze well.

banoffee pie shots

4 digestive biscuits/graham
  crackers, crumbled
20 g/1 generous tablespoon
  unsalted butter, melted
225 g/½ lb. store-bought
  caramel
2 ripe bananas
250 ml/1 generous cup
  double/heavy cream

2 tablespoons cream cheese
1 teaspoon caster/superfine
  sugar
chocolate chips, to decorate

10 shot glasses

Makes 10

Put the biscuit/cracker crumbs in a bowl and stir in the melted butter. Put a heaped teaspoon of the mixture into the base of each shot glass and compact it slightly. Spoon a teaspoon of caramel on top, followed by a tablespoon of the chopped banana.

Put the cream into a bowl and add the sugar and cream cheese. Whisk to soft peaks. Top the bananas with the cream and then sprinkle on the chocolate chips. Refrigerate until ready to serve.

speculoos mousse

Speculoos is a Belgian spiced cookie spread. I was almost too embarrassed to publish such a simple recipe, but it is just too delicious to leave out! Thank you Georgie, the first of my friends to try this little pot and give me the go ahead to unashamedly put it in my book. This isn't a true mousse but I take such pleasure in announcing the words 'speculoos mousse' to friends.

400 g/14 oz. smooth Speculoos
  spread, such as Lotus spread
800 ml/3½ cups double/heavy cream
3 speculoos biscuits/cookies or
  digestive biscuits/graham
  crackers, crumbled, to decorate

20–25 shot glasses

Makes 20–25

Put the speculoos spread and cream into a large bowl.

Use an electric hand-held whisk to mix until thick. You should be able to see the beater marks through the cream.

Spoon the mousse into shot glasses and top with the crushed speculoos biscuits/cookies. Serve.

If you are preparing the mousses in advance, cover with clingfilm/plastic wrap and chill, adding the crumbled biscuits/crackers just before serving.

pomegranate molasses fruit salad

500 g/1 lb. 2 oz. mixed
  fruit, such as bananas,
  blueberries, strawberries
  and pomegranate
  seeds, chilled
freshly squeezed juice of
  1 orange

1–2 tablespoons
  pomegranate molasses

15 shot glasses

Makes 15

Dice the fruit finely and place in a large bowl. (Leave small items such as blueberries and pomegranate seeds whole.) Squeeze over the orange juice.

Add 1 tablespoon of pomegranate molasses and toss to mix. Taste and add more molasses, if necessary. Spoon into individual shot glasses. Serve.

lemon posset with thyme crumble

600 ml/2½ cups double/heavy
    cream
150 g/¾ cup caster/granulated
    sugar
grated zest and juice of 2 lemons

For the crumble
40 g/scant ½ cup rolled/
    old-fashioned oats
20 g/1½ tablespoons unsalted
    butter, softened
20 g/1 tablespoon plus 2 teaspoons
    demerara/raw sugar
half a pinch of sea salt
2 sprigs of thyme, leaves picked
    off the stalk

15 shot glasses

Makes 15

Pour the cream into a saucepan and bring to a gentle simmer over low heat. Add the sugar and stir until dissolved, then continue to simmer for a few minutes to let the cream thicken slightly.

Whisk in the zest and juice of the lemons.

Pour the mixture into a jug/pitcher and stand in a bowl of iced water to cool down, stirring every minute or so to prevent a skin from forming.

When cooled a little, pour into shot glasses and set in the refrigerator for at least 1 hour.

For the crumble, preheat oven to 200°C (400°F) Gas 6.

In a mixing bowl, mix together the oats, softened butter, sugar and salt, and then spread the crumble mixture out on a baking sheet.

Bake in the preheated oven for 10 minutes, then stir the crumble gently and add the thyme. Return to the oven for 5–10 minutes more, until the oats are crunchy. Remove from the oven and allow to cool.

Sprinkle the crumble topping onto the possets and serve.

white chocolate & cointreau tiramisù

300 ml/1¼ cups strong
    espresso coffee
13 sponge fingers (about 100 g/
    3½ oz.)
100 g/3½ oz. good-quality
    white chocolate
250 g/9 oz. mascarpone
2 eggs, separated
150 ml/scant ⅔ cup double/
    heavy cream
1½ tablespoons Cointreau
unsweetened cocoa powder,
    to decorate

15 shot glasses

Makes 15

Pour the coffee into a shallow dish. Dip five of the sponge fingers in the coffee, one at a time, for 3 seconds on each side and then break each finger into 3. Place each third into the base of each glass.

Melt the chocolate in a bowl set over hot water in a saucepan, taking care that the water is not in contact with the bowl. Allow to cool. Once cool, add the mascarpone and then the egg yolks. Whisk to combine. Pour over the cream and the Cointreau and whisk again to combine.

In a clean bowl, whisk the egg whites until they hold stiff peaks. Gently fold the whites into the mascarpone mix. Spoon a heaped tablespoon of the mixture into each glass, covering the sponge finger.

Dip the remaining sponge fingers in the coffee, one at a time, for 3 seconds on each side and then break each finger in half. Press one into each glass. (There will be one half left over, which you can discard or eat!)

Top the glasses with the remaining mascarpone mix and chill for at least 1 hour. When ready to serve, sift a little cocoa on top.

Overleaf, from left to right: banoffee pie shots (p122), speculoos mousse (p122), pomegranate molasses fruit salad (p122), lemon posset with thyme crumble (p123), white chocolate & cointreau tiramisù (p123).

mini pavlovas

Although they only take 20 minutes to bake, it's best to leave meringues to dry out in the oven for a few hours. For this reason, I tend to leave them as my last job of the day. They're a great thing to do ahead of time as you can keep them in an airtight container for 2 weeks. The coulis is optional – they are still lovely without it. Sometimes I'll whisk a drop of rose water into the cream for a little extra flavour.

300 ml/1¼ cups double/
*   heavy cream*
300 g/10½ oz. mixed berries,
*   sliced into small pieces*

For the meringue
red food colouring, optional
2 egg whites
a pinch of salt
120 g/⅔ cup caster/superfine
*   sugar*

For the raspberry coulis
150 g/1 cup raspberries
freshly squeezed juice of ½
*   a lemon*
1 tablespoon icing/
*   confectioners' sugar*

a baking sheet, lined with a silicone mat
a piping/pastry bag
small paintbrush
food colouring (optional)

Makes 40–45

Preheat the oven to 140°C (275°F) Gas 1.

If you wish to colour your meringues, paint 8 stripes of food colouring inside the piping bag from the tip, halfway up the bag. Set aside.

Use an electric hand-held whisk to slowly whisk the egg whites with a pinch of salt on medium speed in a clean bowl, until they are frothy.

Gradually add the sugar, a teaspoonful at a time, while increasing the speed of the whisk to high. Once all the sugar has been added and the meringue is shiny, holds its shape and is not grainy, fill the piping bag.

Make sure there are no air bubbles. Twist the piping bag and snip the end off, 2.5 cm/1 in. from the tip.

Pipe the meringue to a diameter of 2.5 cm/1 in., leaving a 2.5-cm/1-in. space between them. They will expand slightly when baked.

Put the meringues in the oven and immediately turn the temperature down to 120°C (250°F) Gas ½. It is important that you do not open the door to the oven until the meringues are baked. Bake for 20 minutes, switch the oven off and leave the meringues inside to dry out overnight or for at least 2 hours.

To make the coulis, place the raspberries in a small saucepan and squeeze over the lemon juice.

Heat the raspberries over a gentle heat, crushing them with a fork as they heat up. Stir in the icing/confectioners' sugar.

Let the mixture simmer for a minute or so, then remove the saucepan from the heat. Blend the mixture in a food processor or blender, then sieve/strain it and let cool.

Whisk the cream until stiff. Top the meringues with the cream and berries up to 30 minutes before serving. Drizzle with coulis just before serving.

lemon & lime meringue tarts

This is a little twist on the classic lemon meringue pie. I have added lime to the traditional lemon filling, and topped it with a gooey, not-quite-set meringue. It's a little fun and messy, perhaps best for an informal occasion!

125 g/1 cup plain/all-purpose
    flour
45 g/3 tablespoons unsalted butter
50 g/½ cup icing/confectioners'
    sugar
1 egg
a pinch of salt

For the filling
45 g/3 tablespoons unsalted butter
80 ml/⅓ cup double/heavy cream
1 egg
3 egg yolks
80 g/generous ⅓ cup caster/
    granulated sugar
4 tablespoons lemon juice
2 tablespoons lime juice
grated zest of 1 lemon and 1 lime

For the meringue
2 egg whites
120 g/scant ⅔ cup caster/
    superfine sugar
1 teaspoon cornflour/
    cornstarch

a piping/pastry bag
a 24-hole mini muffin pan,
greased
a 6-cm/2½-in. pastry/cookie
cutter
a chef's blowtorch (optional)

Makes 30 approx

Preheat the oven to 180°C (350°F) Gas 4.

To make the pastry, place all of the ingredients in a food processor, and pulse until combined.

Tip the dough out onto a lightly floured surface and knead a couple of times, wrap in clingfilm/plastic wrap and refrigerate for 2 hours.

Roll out the pastry to 3 mm/⅛ in. thick and then stamp out disks with the cutter. Carefully press them down into the muffin pan holes and bake for 9–10 minutes, or until golden and cooked on the bottom. Cool on a wire rack.

To make the filling, melt the butter in a small pan. Add the cream, stir well, take off the heat and put aside.

Whisk the eggs and sugar together, place in a bowl set over a saucepan of hot water (the bowl and water should not come into contact) and stir for a few minutes. Add the lemon and lime juice, zests, cream and butter mix and stir well. Continue to cook, whilst stirring with a spatula until the mixture thickens – about 5 minutes. Set aside to cool.

To make the meringue, whisk the egg whites in a clean bowl with an electric hand-held whisk until they reach the frothy soft-peak stage. Slowly add the sugar while continuing to whisk. When the meringue is glossy and stiff, whisk in the cornflour/cornstarch and then transfer to a piping/pastry bag.

Fill each tart case with a teaspoonful of the filling. Pipe the meringue on top.

Using a chef's blowtorch, brown the sides and leave to cool. (If you do not have a chef's blowtorch, you can brown the meringues in the oven at 200°C (400°F) Gas 6. The meringues will take only a few minutes to brown, so check them regularly. The meringue will grow considerably in the oven, so only pipe a small amount on each tart.)

Serve immediately, or chill for a few hours until you are ready to serve.

raspberry & lime cheesecakes

250 g/9 oz. digestive
  biscuits/graham crackers,
  blitzed to crumbs in a
  food processor
125 g/1 stick plus 1
  tablespoon unsalted
  butter, melted
½ teaspoon ground
  cinnamon
½ teaspoon ground ginger
  (optional)
a pinch of salt
250 g/9 oz. white chocolate
275 ml/1 generous cup
  double/heavy cream

500 g/18 oz. full-fat cream
  cheese
150 g/5½ oz. ricotta
5 gelatine leaves, soaked
  in cold water for
  5–10 minutes
grated zest of 1 lime
300 g/11 oz. raspberries

20 x 30-cm/8 x 12-in.
brownie pan, lined with
baking parchment

Makes 35

Place the biscuit/cracker crumbs into a bowl and mix in the melted butter, spices and salt. Put into the prepared pan and flatten to make the base. Chill.

Melt the chocolate with 150 ml/⅔ cup of the cream in a saucepan over low heat. Transfer to a large bowl and add the cream cheese, ricotta and zest. Whisk.

Squeeze out any excess water from the gelatine. Heat the remaining cream in a small saucepan to simmering point, take off the heat and whisk in the gelatine. Add to the cheese mixture and whisk well.

Set aside 35 raspberries for decoration, then arrange the remaining raspberries over the base. Pour in the cheesecake mixture. Cover in clingfilm/plastic wrap and place in the refrigerator to set overnight.

To serve, use a sharp knife to cut the cheesecake into 35 squares, then top each with a raspberry.

piña colada jellies

I saw the idea for 'broken-glass jello' on justjennrecipes.com and couldn't wait to make a boozy version.

690 ml/scant 3 cups pineapple
  juice (not from concentrate)
34 sheets of gelatine, softened in
  cold water for 5–10 minutes
345 ml/1½ cups cherry juice
400 g /14 oz. sweetened
  condensed milk
300 ml/1¼ cups Malibu or other
  coconut-flavoured white rum
80 ml/⅓ cup coconut cream

25 x 18-cm/10 x 7-in.
and 12 x 9-cm/4½ x 3½-in.
containers, lined with
clingfilm/plastic wrap

Makes about 120 cubes

Heat 120 ml/½ cup pineapple juice to a simmer in a saucepan. Take off the heat, squeeze the water out of 11 sheets of gelatine, add to the juice and whisk. Add this to the remaining pineapple juice and whisk. Pour into the large prepared container and set in the refrigerator for at least 3 hours.

Heat 60 ml/¼ cup of the cherry juice to a simmer in a saucepan. Take off the heat, squeeze the water out of 6 sheets of gelatine, add to the juice and whisk. Add this to the remaining cherry juice and whisk. Pour into the small prepared container and set in the refrigerator for at least 3 hours.

Once both jellies are set, heat 180 ml/¾ cup water to a simmer in a saucepan. Take off the heat. Squeeze the water out of 17 sheets of gelatine, add to the water and whisk. Add this to the condensed milk, along with the Malibu, 150 ml/generous ½ cup water and the coconut cream. Mix then let cool but not set.

Cut the pineapple and cherry jellies into 1.5-cm/¾-in. cubes. Arrange the cubes in a container large enough to hold them all, then cover with the cooled coconut jelly to a depth of 2.5 cm/1 in. Set in the refrigerator overnight. The next day, cut into 2.5-cm/1-in. cubes to serve.

This page: lemon & lime meringue tarts (p128), raspberry lime cheesecakes (p129).
Opposite: piña colada jellies (p129).

churros

A churro dunked in thick hot chocolate was a weekend treat for us as kids. Now, I'll happily order them on their own and sneak a dunk into my café con leche. Perfect churros come with practice. The exterior should be crisp and the inside chewy but light with air pockets. If you do not have a thermometer, measure 200 ml/scant 1 cup boiling water with 60 ml/4 tablespoons cold water. Thank you, Juan, for the recipe.

½ teaspoon salt
200 g/1⅔ cups strong white/
* bread flour*
¼ teaspoon bicarbonate of soda/
* baking soda*
260 ml/generous 1 cup water at
* around 70° C (160°F)*
400 ml/1¾ cups sunflower/corn oil
* for frying*

For the dipping sauce
100 g/3½ oz. dark/bittersweet
* (70%) chocolate, chopped*
120 ml/½ cup double/heavy cream

a thermometer
a piping/pastry bag

Makes 30 approx

Whisk the salt, flour and bicarbonate of soda in a bowl. Add the water and whisk quite vigorously so that there are no lumps.

Leave to sit in the bowl for 5–10 minutes, or until cooled and thickened slightly, while you prepare the oil.

Heat the oil in a small saucepan and bring to 180°C (350°F).

Spoon the dough into a piping/pastry bag (use a star nozzle/tip if you want ridges). Twist the piping/pastry bag and hold with one hand. Gently squeeze out the dough to a 5-cm/2-in. piece and snip with scissors into the oil, frying in small batches.

Fry for a couple of minutes and then turn over with tongs and cook until golden brown. Drain on paper towels and keep the churros in a warm oven.

There is no strict shape for churros. Snipping them into the hot oil in lines is the easiest way to get started. Once you get the hang of it, you can try piping them into other shapes, such as the horseshoes shown.

For the dipping sauce, place the chopped chocolate in a heatproof bowl. Bring the double/heavy cream to a simmer in a saucepan, then pour over the chocolate. Let it sit for 1 minute, then stir to combine. Serve the churros immediately, accompanied by the dipping sauce.

malaysian coconut pancakes

I have been cooking for May's Malaysian Supperclubs at my home over the last year.
May has introduced me to so many ingredients that I now feel at home in the Chinese
supermarket. One of my favourite discoveries is Gula Melaka (Malaysian palm sugar)
It's sold in solid blocks and when melted, tastes like a rich, dark caramel. Here it
transforms desiccated coconut, into a soft, sticky stuffing for a coconut pancake.

In Malaysia these are made with pandan leaves and are coloured green, so my recipe
isn't too authentic, but it is delicious and moreish. You can make the filling days in
advance, kept wrapped well in the refrigerator.

80 g/½ cup Gula Melaka
  (palm sugar/jaggery)
150 g/5 oz. desiccated/dried
  unsweetened shredded coconut

For the pancake batter
120 g/4 oz.coconut cream
1 egg
150 g/1¼ cups plain/all-purpose
  flour
a pinch of salt
40 g/3 tablespoons unsalted
  butter

20-cm/8-in. crêpe pan or
frying pan/skillet

Makes 24

Melt the palm sugar with 100 ml/scant ½ cup water in a saucepan over
a low heat until it has dissolved. Pour over the desiccated coconut and
mix well with a spoon. Cover and set aside.

To make the pancakes, whisk together the coconut cream, egg and
260 ml/1¼ cup water in a jug/pitcher.

Put the flour and salt in a large bowl and make a well in the centre.
Pour the liquid mixture into the centre and whisk, slowly incorporating
the flour from all the sides. When all is incorporated, whisk well.

Now is the time to add a little more water if the pancake batter is too
thick, but you do want a thicker batter than you would do for a crêpe.

Heat the pan and melt the butter. Pour half into the batter and half
onto a saucer to use with a paper towel to grease the pan later.

Pour in half a ladleful of batter and swirl it around the pan. When small
bubbles appear, flip the pancake over and cook the other side for
another minute or so. Transfer to a plate.

Repeat with the rest of the batter. When all the pancakes are cooked,
add a heaped tablespoonful of the coconut mix into the bottom centre
of each pancake. Roll halfway, tightly tuck in the sides and roll into a
log. Slice on the diagonal into 2 portions to serve.

banana, hazelnut & cream pancakes

These feather-light pancakes with their crisp edges make the perfect pockets for warm caramelized bananas, chocolate-hazelnut spread and cream. You can make the batter the day before, but the bananas need to be made close to serving or the crunchy top will melt.

1 large banana, sliced

50 g/¼ cup caster/granulated sugar

50 g/generous ⅓ cup plain/
all-purpose flour

a pinch of salt

1 egg

100 ml /scant ½ cup
semi-skimmed milk

1 tablespoon butter

120 g/4 oz. chocolate-hazelnut
spread, such as Nutella

100 ml/scant ½ cup crème
fraîche/sour cream

20-cm/8-in. crêpe pan or
frying pan/skillet

a chef's blowtorch (optional)

Makes 12

To caramelize the bananas, lay the banana pieces on a baking sheet. Sprinkle over the sugar and use a blowtorch to caramelize the tops. Alternatively, use an overhead grill/broiler. Leave to cool.

To make the pancakes, sift the flour and salt into a bowl and make a well in the centre. Beat the egg with the milk and slowly pour it into the well as you whisk in the flour from the sides. Add a splash of water until you have the consistency of single/light cream.

Melt the butter in the pan and whisk it into the pancake mix.

Return the pan to a medium heat and add a small ladle of mix to the pan, quickly swirling it around the edges so that you have a very thin coating. Pour any excess back into the batter bowl.

After a minute or so, flip the pancake over with a spatula and cook for a further 10 seconds, or until golden.

You can keep the pancakes warm in a low oven under a kitchen towel.

When all pancakes are cooked, cut them in half. Lay them out on a board and add a teaspoon each of nutella and crème fraîche, and a couple of slices of banana. Roll them tightly into cones and serve.

buttermilk doughnuts

1 egg

130 ml/½ cup buttermilk

200 g/1½ cups self-raising/
self-rising flour

a pinch of salt

a pinch of ground cinnamon

20 g/1 tablespoon unsalted butter

20 g/1 tablespoon plus 1
teaspoon caster/granulated
sugar, plus extra for rolling

vegetable oil, for deep-frying

Makes 15

Put the oil for deep-frying into a saucepan and heat to 170°C (340°F).

In a small bowl, whisk together the egg and buttermilk. In a large bowl, mix the flour, salt and cinnamon together. Rub in the butter with your fingertips, then mix in the sugar. Add the buttermilk mixture, and quickly bring the mixture together with a spoon. Tip the wet dough out onto a floured surface, gather into a ball and flour the top. Roll out the dough to 2.5 cm/1 in. thick. Stamp out rounds with a 4-cm/1½-in. cutter or shot glass. With floured hands, lightly roll them into balls.

Drop the balls into the hot oil, in batches, and cook for about 4 minutes, turning them over every minute or so, until cooked through.

Roll them in a shallow bowl of sugar and serve warm.

This page: malaysian coconut pancakes (p134),
banana, hazelnut & cream pancakes (p135).
Opposite: buttermilk doughnuts (p135).

menu planners

These menu planners will help you put together a canapé menu for a party whatever the occasion. I have suggested 11 canapés for each menu, along with two sweet bites that can replace a couple of the savoury choices, if you prefer. These are just a few suggestions – feel free to mix and match throughout the book as much as you like!

Formal drinks party
blue cheese, pear & walnut blinis 36
courgette & parmesan blinis 37
squash frittatas with pea purée & roasted
  tomatoes 37
quail's eggs, crayfish & caviar blinis 54
baba ganoush & feta endives 99
smoked salmon, enoki & white miso cucumber
  boats 74
sea bass ceviche, lychee & chilli 104
seared beef fillet with horseradish 56
crostini with truffled wild mushrooms 46
honey soy mackerel & daikon maki 71
scallops in pancetta 41
raspberry & lime cheesecakes 129
frangelico truffles 120

Casual drinks party
smoked mackerel, apple & fennel on rye 50
anise crackers, goat's cheese, honey & thyme 44
spinach, fennel & cumin ricotta cakes 64
harissa aubergine fritters 99
sesame prawn toasts 76
chilli devilled eggs 76
chilli con carne empanadillas 112
tortilla 32
butternut squash & chorizo skewers 32
kofte 94
thai fish cakes 88
white chocolate & cointreau tiramisu 123
portuguese custard tarts 117

Festive winter drinks party
chestnuts & bacon 46
duck breast chinese pancakes with ginger
  jammy plums 78
persian sausage rolls 94
moroccan chicken puffs 95
borek with mint & honey 98
tandoori prawns 64
spicy salmon skewers 60
pea & potato samosas 65
crostini with truffled wild mushrooms 46
leek & parmesan filo tartlets 46
empanadillas 112
speculoos mousse 122
chestnut & chocolate baskets 116

Summer drinks party
bocconcini skewers 40
jerk chicken & plantain skewers 106
watermelon, feta, basil & balsamic 40
mediterranean vegetable crostini with
  pesto 29
jamaican-spiced prawn & mango skewers 106
black bean quesadillas 108
gazpacho 28
crab, mango & avocado rolls 80
asian slaw & prawn tarts 90
gochujang chicken skewers 84
pulled pork on cornbread muffins 108
mini pavlovas 126
piña colada jellies 129

Cooking for vegetarians?

The following recipes are all meat-free:

romesco dip 12

guacamole 12

beetroot hummus 13

tzatziki 16

roast carrot, ginger & miso dip 16

tortilla chips 16

black bean hummus 17

marinated feta 17

spicy popcorn 20

stilton & walnut biscuits 20

cayenne & cheddar biscuits 21

madras cheddar biscuits 21

ajo blanco 28

tortilla 32

squash frittatas 37

bocconcini skewers 40

watermelon feta, basil & balsamic 40

asparagus filo cigars 41

crackers with cashew pâté, sun-dried tomatoes & dill 44

anise crackers, goat's cheese, honey & thyme 44

crostini with truffled wild mushrooms 46

beetroot, cucumber & apple on crispbread 50

beetroot, dill & goat's cheese cups 56

onion bhajis 61

pani puri 61

spinach, fennel & cumin ricotta cakes 64

pea & potato samosas 65

tofu, ginger & lime spoons 74

chilli devilled eggs 76

yee sang rolls 81

miso-glazed aubergine skewers 86

borek with mint & honey 98

baba ganoush & feta endives 99

dates stuffed with goat's cheese, pistachios
& pomegranate 99

harissa aubergine fritters 99

black bean quesadillas 108

(Check the packaging of cheeses to ensure they are
suitable for vegetarians. Desserts containing gelatine
are not suitable for vegetarians.)

Looking for gluten-free recipes?

Try a selection from the following:

tortilla 32

squash frittatas 37

watermelon, feta, basil & balsamic 40

bocconcini skewers 40

artichoke, mozzarella & speck 40

spicy salmon skewers 60

chicken tikka skewers 60

tandoori prawns 64

spiced coconut lamb skewers 65

chilli devilled eggs 76

crabstick & avocado maki 71

honey soy mackerel & daikon maki 71

pickled mackerel compressed sushi

smoked salmon, enoki & white miso
cucumber boats 74

tofu, ginger & lime spoons 74

tuna, daikon & wasabi rolls 80

crab, mango & avocado rolls 80

yee sang rolls 81

gochujang chicken skewers 84

coconut calamari 88

thai fish cakes 88

kofte 94

za'atar roast chicken & sumac labneh
lettuce cups 95

baba ganoush & feta endives 99

dates stuffed with goat's cheese, pistachios
& pomegranate 99

tequila scallops 104

sea bass ceviche, lychee & chilli 104

tuna & wasabi ceviche 104

jamaican-spiced prawn & mango skewers 106

jerk chicken & plantain skewers 106

chocolate & almond raspberry cakes 117

chocolate & espresso pots 116

frangelico truffles 120

pomegranate molasses fruit salad 122

lemon posset 123

mini pavlovas 126

piña colada jellies 129

suppliers

UK

Sous Chef
Fantastic online shop selling everything from gochujang to okonomiyaki sauce
www.souschef.co.uk
delivers to Europe

Green Saffron
The most wonderful farm-fresh Indian spices and spice blends
www.greensaffron.com

Nisbets
Kitchen equipment, next day delivery
www.nisbets.co.uk

Spikomat
Huge range of skewers and presentation items
www.skewers.co.uk

Japan Centre
Great range of Japanese ingredients and tableware
www.japancentre.com

Talad Thai Supermarket
For fresh tofu and a range of Asian ingredients
326 Upper Richmond Rd, London SW15 6TL
020 8789 8084

SeeWoo Foods
Oriental food specialists
www.seewoo.com

Wing of St Mawes
Cornish fishmongers delivering top-quality fish and seafood
www.wingofstmawes.co.uk

R. Garcia and Sons
The top supplier of Spanish food in London
www.rgarciaandsons.com

Parsons Nose Butcher
Top-quality, friendly butchers
www.parsonsnose.co.uk

Il Mulino Bakery
Great for miniatures – everything from mini bagels to mini brioche
Unit 8, Lyndon Yard, Riverside Road, Wimbledon, SW17 0BA

Isle of Wight tomatoes
Flavoursome tomatoes
www.thetomatostall.co.uk

Wholegood
Fresh, seasonal organic fruit and vegetables
www.wholegood.co.uk

Marky Market
Order your meat and fish from Mark and he will go to Billingsgate and Smithfield while you sleep, and deliver or meet you in London, later the same day
www.markymarket.com

US

Whole Foods
www.wholefoodsmarket.com

Trader Joe's
www.traderjoes.com

Amigo Foods
Foods from Spain including chorizo and Serrano ham
www.amigofoods.com

Mountain Rose Herbs
Online shop selling high-quality herbs and spices
www.mountainroseherbs.com

Organic Spices
Online shop selling organic herbs and spices
www.organicspices.com

McCall's Meat and Fish Company
Market selling premium meat and fish in Los Angeles
www.mccallsmeatandfish.com
2117 Hillhurst Avenue, Los Angeles, CA 90027

New Mexican Connection
Fresh and dried New Mexican favourites
www.newmexicanconnection.com

index

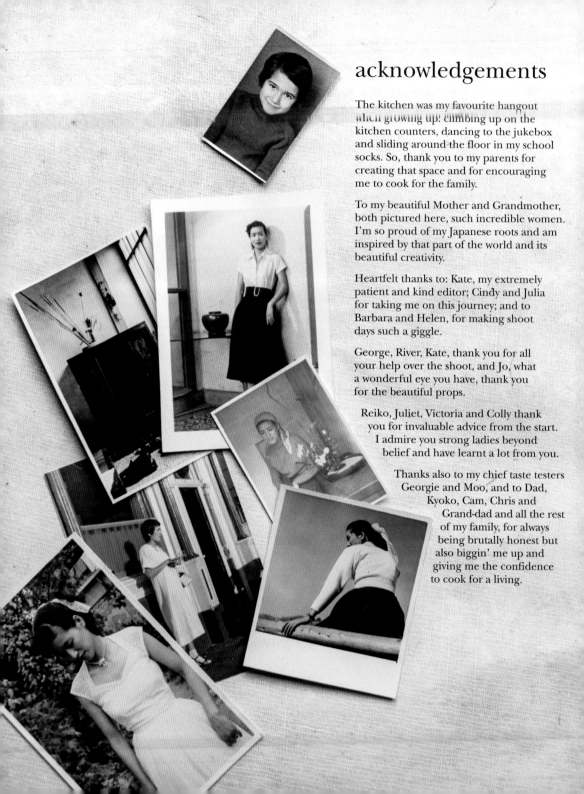

acknowledgements

The kitchen was my favourite hangout when growing up! climbing up on the kitchen counters, dancing to the jukebox and sliding around the floor in my school socks. So, thank you to my parents for creating that space and for encouraging me to cook for the family.

To my beautiful Mother and Grandmother, both pictured here, such incredible women. I'm so proud of my Japanese roots and am inspired by that part of the world and its beautiful creativity.

Heartfelt thanks to: Kate, my extremely patient and kind editor; Cindy and Julia for taking me on this journey; and to Barbara and Helen, for making shoot days such a giggle.

George, River, Kate, thank you for all your help over the shoot, and Jo, what a wonderful eye you have, thank you for the beautiful props.

Reiko, Juliet, Victoria and Colly thank you for invaluable advice from the start. I admire you strong ladies beyond belief and have learnt a lot from you.

Thanks also to my chief taste testers Georgie and Moo, and to Dad, Kyoko, Cam, Chris and Grand-dad and all the rest of my family, for always being brutally honest but also biggin' me up and giving me the confidence to cook for a living.